NO STON

LEFT UNTURNED

NO STONE LEFT UNTURNED

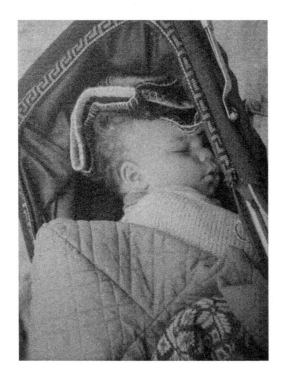

A relentless pursuit of the truth to uncover biological parentage

Colin Curruthers

Contents

Acknowledgements

Firstly, I would like to thank my wife for supporting me every step of the way with my biological search and for encouraging me to write this memoir. I'd also like to thank family members and friends who have supported me at different stages of the search journey. Finally, special thanks to new acquaintances I met during this search, who have continued to give me the impetus to see this journey through. I couldn't have achieved this without you all.

Preface

This is an intimate account of an adult adoptee's journey as he spent many years searching for his biological parents. The account captures his thoughts, emotions and physical encounters whilst on this journey, combined with wider recollections which are thought to be correlated to the adoption experience. It is hoped the account will provide support, comfort and inspiration to those thinking of searching for their biological parents and those who have already started out on this journey. The names of the individuals involved, along with the organisations and locations which feature, have been changed to protect anonymity.

Introduction

I was adopted in October 1968. I was given this information by my adoptive parents, probably when I was eight or nine years old. I can't remember my exact age as it wasn't something I made a note of at the time. *"Your birth parents were too old to look after you"* was the reason specified by my adoptive parents for being given up. I don't recall being sad or upset at the time. I just felt special, as according to my adoptive parents, I had been the child they chose. This sense of feeling special sadly didn't last forever and altered as I moved towards adolescence. It did make me think about who these "elderly" people were who had been too old to look after me. Being adopted was never really spoken about again. It didn't stop me wondering, though.

To an outsider, it was probably quite obvious I wasn't part of my natural family. My heavy mop of ginger hair was a giveaway. I simply didn't look like anyone else in the family. As I grew older, I didn't share any physical features, interests or personality traits, either. To avoid upsetting my adoptive parents and maintain the illusion of a "natural" family, I seemed to become a clone of them, especially for the first 16 years of my life, anyway. From this point onwards, the introduction of alcohol and interest in things such as gambling began to take me down a different path. I knew these types of pastimes were foreign to my adoptive parents and would be frowned upon, so I tried my best to keep them well concealed.

Although I was constantly on the lookout for someone who looked like me, I never really encountered anyone. This lack of personal identity precluded me from having a sense of belonging. This was followed by two key questions: "where do I fit in?" and "where do I come from?"

My biological mother: Glenda Alice Curruthers

CHAPTER ONE

Searching for Mother

On the face of it, 29 June 1994 was just another day. But I didn't know what I was going to stumble into. Before I delve into this fully, I feel I should provide an explanation of events leading up to this day.

In March 1994, I was in the first year of a BTEC Diploma in Leisure Studies. Prior to this, I had worked in the textile industry for nine years. During this nine-year period, I was in a bubble. I didn't have to tax myself too much and led a pretty sheltered life. Living at home with my adoptive parents, I didn't have too much responsibility either. It's fair to say that leaving industry and attending a College of Further Education changed my life for the better. It gave me a fresh challenge. It enabled me to meet new people and make new friends. It gave me a chance to visit new places. But most importantly, I became more confident and became more inquisitive about things around me. This included my adoption and a desire to understand my biological heritage. Who exactly were the people responsible for bringing me into this world back in 1968? I was curious and wanted to know more.

It's at this point I'd like to mention my then girlfriend, and now wife, who's been a fantastic support during the journey I have been on. I know deep down it has driven her mad at times and she has probably wanted to change the record or stop the search and call it a day. To her credit, she's never muttered those words and always offered sound advice and words of encouragement throughout.

One of the things I pondered on commencing this journey was the following. Should I inform my adoptive parents of my ancestry challenge? It didn't take too long to decide that this search should remain covert. I thought they wouldn't understand or would become upset, or perhaps even feel betrayed.

Back in the day, having a girlfriend who lived in a different town was handy. Especially when you lived at home and needed a different mailing address for correspondence. Some of the early activity in this search is a bit hazy. After all, there wasn't a roadmap or specific pathway to follow. I wish there was. To be brutally honest, there are lots of barriers, dead ends, rejections, confusion, frustration and emotional ups and downs. For those who follow a similar path, you are going to need to protect yourself along the way or you'll get hurt. One way to protect yourself from the effects is to have low expectations of the search, which is easier said than done. That's my experience, anyway. Let the search begin.

Information contained in the certificate of birth I had at the time was limited. It only covered Name; Sex; Date of Birth and Place of Birth. I realised that this information wasn't going to assist me in my search, and I needed more. My first encounter with any form of adoption support agency happened in April 1994. I would have been 26 at the time. Little did I know how long the journey would take and, more importantly, what the outcome would be. In my initial meeting at the local Social Services office, the social worker advised me to send off for my original birth certificate to the General Register Office in Southport. I was told that on receipt of this document, I should return to the Social Services office for a second meeting, which they described as a counselling session. This is where a different mailing address came in handy. Within a week, I had an official-looking letter postmarked Southport, Merseyside.

What the heck is this? They've sent me the wrong birth certificate. This is for somebody called Colin Curruthers, rather than Peter Jackson. Then the penny dropped. The lady at Social Services had mentioned it was likely I'd had a different name when I was born. I tried to calm down to look at this more closely. The document contained a few details, which I read carefully: Name: Colin Curruthers; Mother: Glenda Alice Curruthers; Address: 196 Mayo Lane, Littleborough, Rochdale, Greater Manchester; Father: Unknown... Oh my goodness. I didn't know what to make of this, but it didn't feel good. I was totally confused.

The second meeting with Social Services soon came around. The information relayed to me in the counselling session is all a bit hazy now. But I expect it covered advice on the pitfalls of searching for one's birth parents and scenarios of what the potential outcome could be. That's if there was an outcome to this search. I do remember at the end of the meeting I was given options as to the way forward. I could explore my biological heritage further on my own or receive arbitrator support via their mediation service.

I knew before leaving the building which option I was taking. And it wasn't going down the mediation route. I had a new lease of life. I was cruising through my college course with distinctions coming out of my ears. Confidence was sky-high. The depressing world of textiles was but a distant memory. I had respect from my college peers. I knew best. Why should I listen to these people? My tactic was to get to the bottom of this as soon as possible. Nobody said I couldn't do this. I needed to find this Glenda Curruthers and find out what the heck had gone on back in 1968. And while I was at it, I was determined to find out why it stated "Father: Unknown".

The information contained in the recently acquired birth certificate played on my mind. *I need to explore this further*, I thought.

Let's drive to the address provided. It won't do any harm, will it? A few days later, on a wet Sunday evening, my girlfriend and I pulled up outside 196 Mayo Lane, Littleborough. The house didn't look anything special, probably ex-council stock. What was the plan? The plan was to march up to the house, knock on the door and see how far I got. We sat there for a few minutes just staring at the house. Nerves kicked in and I didn't have the bottle to go through with it. We drove the 20 miles or so back to my home address.

Two weeks later, I went back and parked up on Mayo Lane. It was the afternoon of 29 June 1994. I set off from home with the intention of visiting the library in Rochdale to search the electoral records. That would inform me of who lived at the address. It was all going to plan when I received a message. This wasn't a mobile phone message as I didn't own one at the time. It was a message from the abyss into my brain. It said: "Don't bother going to the library. Just go to the house." I don't normally act on impulse, but I did on that occasion. I wasn't prepared for what happened next.

I didn't bottle it this time. Far from it. At this late stage, I wondered whether I could find out who lived in the house before knocking on the door. It was a lovely sunny afternoon. Across the road, a man was tending his garden. I walked over. "Who lives at 196?" I asked. He wasn't suspicious about my question. "That'll be old Jack," he shouted back. At that point, I didn't stop to think who old Jack could be. Nor did I ask any more questions. Undeterred, I walked towards the house and knocked on the door. I was nervous, though.

A tall, elderly man answered the door. I came straight out with it. "I'm looking for someone who used to live here in 1968. She was called Glenda Alice Curruthers." His demeanour altered immediately. He went from defensive to ultra-defensive in a split second. "Who are you?" he asked. "I'm Peter Jackson. I don't want to cause any trouble. I'm looking for my biological mother. She was called Glenda and she lived here in 1968." He paused. I knew I was onto something, but what? He stared at me for what seemed an eternity. "Show me some ID!"he demanded. I panicked. All I had was my student card. Could I convince him this was a genuine enquiry? I handed him the card. He briefly looked at it but didn't scrutinise it too closely. I reiterated that I wasn't there to cause anyone any problems and if there was a problem, I'd leave. Then he uttered a sentence I'll remember for the rest of my life. "You'd better come in, son." What was going on? And who was this guy?

He led me down the hallway. A wreath of flowers was on the floor, leaning against the wall. I can picture them now. Pink and white roses with a message attached. It didn't register what the wreath might symbolise. I was too busy following this guy. Then came the next instruction. He pointed into a room to the right of the hallway. "Go in there, sit down and don't move." I followed his instruction as he made his way upstairs. By this point, I was rigid with what I can only describe as fright. I was beginning to wonder whether I had done the right thing in taking on this search myself and coming to this house.

I could hear voices upstairs. This was followed by someone coming downstairs at pace. There was no escape now. Whatever was coming in my direction I would have to tackle head-on. An elderly woman with snowy white hair burst into the room. The old man was a couple of paces behind her. She ran towards me. She was hysterical. She placed her hands on my face, then repeated the phrase "He's been sent from God" over and over again. I didn't say anything. I was caught up in this whirlwind of activity and emotion. I just went with it. I still didn't know who she was. Then came the questions. One after another. Lots of them. "What's your name? Where do you live? How have you found us? How long have you been looking for us? Do your parents know you are here? What was your adoption like?" And so on. She was so excited that she didn't give me a chance to answer them. Then the hysterics started again as she recounted how she had been waiting years for this momentous event and only God could have brought us together. Then suddenly she stopped talking. There was a look of horror on her face. She looked across at the elderly man (who had remained quiet since coming into the room). "He doesn't know, does he?" She held my hand tightly. I remember her hands being cold. "Glenda is dead," she said. "She died in 1970. She took her own life. Today is the anniversary of her death. We are going to the crematorium later this afternoon." The death bit didn't register with me. But I was beginning to piece the other information together. I assumed I had just met my biological grandparents on my mother's side. This explained the reason for the wreath in the hallway.... they were going to the crematorium that afternoon. Oh my god, what the hell was happening? The exact detail of the remainder of that visit has escaped my memory. It was a surreal encounter. We probably had a cup of tea or something. I do remember the old lady asking whether she could tell her family and friends that I had turned up out of the blue. I didn't have a problem with that. I drove away from the house that afternoon in shock.

After that afternoon, my girlfriend and I visited 196 Mayo Lane as soon as we could. We were introduced to other family members. This included Glenda's brother, his wife and their children. They were all pleasant to us, which was a relief. The conversation during our subsequent visits was mostly around Glenda. From what we were told, I got the impression she had wanted to keep me rather than give me up for adoption, as did the rest of the family. But circumstances hadn't allowed for that. I didn't step up my questioning around this issue as I didn't want to upset the applecart. I just wanted to maintain a friendly relationship. I secretly wanted to ask lots of questions and probe into the whole affair, but I knew I couldn't. They gave me some personal mementos, such as photos and keepsakes from when I was a baby. Some photos included a boyfriend of my mother. Who was he? Was he my father? This matter was never addressed when I was talking with them, but they seemed to think a lot of him. He was her partner at the time I was conceived. He also had a look of me. Despite this, I never found the right opportunity to ask whether he was my father.

In the year 2000, my biological grandmother passed away. She had cancer. As far as I was aware, I was the last person to see her alive. I was asked by the family to be a pallbearer at the funeral. Despite seeing my biological grandparents a few times in the five years or so before she died, it didn't seem right to be asked to be a pallbearer. I felt out of place at the funeral and more so at the wake. *Who's that guy?* I could feel people thinking. Nobody made an effort to talk to me. It was an awkward few hours, and I couldn't wait to leave.

In some ways, visits to 196 Mayo Lane were never the same after that. Although my biological grandfather had a dry sense of humour, he seemed to tolerate our visits rather than embrace them. He had always relied on his wife to hold court during our visits. Now she wasn't there anymore, it was up to him. Conversation was always hard work. We left every visit with his words, "It's been nice to see you again." I'm not convinced he meant it, though.

CHAPTER TWO

Father Unknown

The fact there was no father named on the birth certificate was bothering me. The waves of inquisitiveness were getting bigger. They were no longer rolling gently onto the beach. They were crashing against the coast with incredible force. It was on my mind more than ever before. It was time to explore this properly. For my sanity, if nothing else.

It was now February 2002. We were married, and we had bought our first house in Clitheroe, Lancashire. I contacted the nearest local authority social services department and within days had an appointment with a social worker. She was very professional, seemed genuine and wanted to help when I explained the situation. She had a positive attitude about the challenge ahead. To help me move forward and try to track down my biological father, the first step was to obtain my adoption records.

The adoption records were retrieved. They made grim reading. And it upset me considerably. Up until now, my understanding of the adoption, and events leading up to the adoption, was based on hearsay from my biological grandparents. They said they had wanted to keep me, and I believed it. The black and white version in front of me read differently. Far differently. Content in the adoption papers was blunt and to the point. It was clear my biological mother showed no emotion or love towards me. That hurt. It was also clear the family were not going to take on any responsibility or consider bringing me up. Although I will never know the truth, they didn't seem to try to keep me at all. The sooner I was adopted the better, as far as they were concerned. I was angry at how an innocent baby could be dealt with back then. I was also bitter towards my new biological family for how they had put a spin on their version of events. According to what I was reading, their version of events simply wasn't true.

One of the reasons for retrieving the papers was to ascertain as much information as possible about my potential father. I was in luck. Two males were named in the court paperwork, and accounts of interviews conducted with these individuals were included. Both categorically denied being my father. As part of the interviews in 1968, both men had been required to provide their home address, which was important for the forthcoming search. The social worker had a plan. She explained she was going to write to both individuals and act as an intermediary between me and them. She warned me that this plan had risks; you never knew how people were going to react when you contacted them out of the blue, especially about such a sensitive issue. She also reminded me that the final outcome might not be positive. I was still up for it, and I followed her advice to the letter.

She set me a task: to establish the current addresses of the males listed in the paperwork. It was more than likely that the addresses listed were now outdated. I relished the challenge. My search included scrolling through lists in local history libraries, town halls and other grand buildings holding electoral register data. Individuals with the same names were found, but there were so many of them. I couldn't be 100 per cent sure I had identified the correct individuals. The confidence I had at the beginning of the search was fading fast. I needed a different approach. Could a private investigator help? I approached one who was based in a nearby town. A fee of £85.00 was quoted for the work. Within 24 hours, I had two addresses, one each for the individuals who would be written to. Having the addresses was one thing, but developing a dialogue with them was going to be another matter entirely. Letters were drafted by the social worker and soon on their way. I waited in anticipation.

Within days, I had another appointment with the social worker. She informed me that communication had taken place with both parties. It was bad news. She broke it to me gently. She explained the first individual had been very aggressive and told her not to contact him again. Information received from the second individual was polite and sympathetic, but there was no sign of wanting a dialogue with me to help me resolve the issue of who my biological father was. With regret, the social worker had to close my case. I was frustrated. I couldn't help thinking that one of these individuals had played a key role in bringing me into this world (and probably enjoyed himself in the process) and then walked away and took no responsibility. *You selfish bastard*, I thought.

CHAPTER THREE

Trying to Cope

Some of the wording included in this section has been developed through reading *The Primal Wound: Understanding the adopted child (1993) by Nancy Verrier*. As a result of reading this text, I was able to rationalise my behaviour and thoughts, brought about by my own situation, and put these into context.

Reading the details in the adoption paperwork hit me hard. The bitterness about the whole adoption situation had escalated in my mind. I made the decision not to visit my biological grandfather again. After all, according to the information in the adoption file, he had clearly done nothing to help my cause in 1968. The waves of anger continued, as did the insecurities of adoption, appearing every day at some point to remind me that I was inferior, less confident, less worthy and less important than those around me. Other adoptees who read this may relate to this. In August 2002, my first daughter was born. I felt totally let down by my biological father (whoever that was) and promised myself that I would be a good father and always be there for her. I hope that has been the case. The same applies to my second daughter, who was born in 2009.

Something of interest happened early in 2003 while I was travelling to work. I worked in Manchester at the time. A work colleague informed me of a bomb scare in the city centre. I was advised to wait on the outskirts of the city as it was gridlocked closer to the centre. This seemed sensible advice. How could I pass the time until the bomb scare was over? I knew I was in the vicinity of where one of the men interviewed in the adoption process lived. It was the one who had been aggressive towards the social worker. I could remember the address. It was lodged in my memory. Using my A – Z street map, it didn't take long to find the house. The house was in a cul-de-sac. I parked up outside the house but on the other side of the street. I didn't have the confidence to knock at the door. That was never the plan. I was just hoping to get a glimpse of him. It was a long shot, though. Suddenly, an ambulance came up the street and parked outside the house I was surveying. It was the type of ambulance you would associate with driving someone to and from outpatient clinics, daycare centres and routine hospital admissions. The driver got out and knocked on the door. What was going on? A man came out of the house pushing a lady in a wheelchair. He pushed her up the garden path, onto the street and towards the ambulance. It was him. I recognised him from the photographs given to me by my biological grandmother. His sandy hair had turned white and his stocky physique was less bulky, but it was him alright. I got out of the car and pretended to be speaking to someone on my mobile phone. (I had one by then.) He waited until the ambulance drove away. I got as close to him as possible. I may have even nodded at him. It was a brief moment, but it felt good. I had achieved something, but I don't know what it was. I dined out on that moment for some time afterwards. For some reason, I felt I had gained an advantage. I hadn't really. I still didn't know who my biological father was. I was kidding myself.

As I have discovered since reaching my mid-forties, one of the first steps to coping with being adopted is to recognize that the experience itself leaves lingering problems. Things such as loss, rejection, and lack of identity and intimacy have been pretty standard in my adult life, but I had failed to understand this. I had just ploughed on regardless, thinking that was just the norm for me, without considering the underlying reasons for my behaviour. Now, here I was, in a situation where not only had I been rejected by my biological mother and her family but, later in life, I had faced yet another rejection. This time it was from those in the frame for fathering me.

As had happened many times previously, the issue of shame reared its head. I think this was linked to the belief that I felt unlovable, brought on by this recent episode of further rejection. Other adoptees are probably quite familiar with this feeling. It is the feeling of being the "dreadful baby", the baby who wasn't good enough to keep. Part of this feeling of shame has to do with the feeling of incompleteness which I suffer from. Something is missing. I am not whole or wholesome. But it's more – the belief I'm defective, impaired or fragmented. Often, the search for the mother is an attempt to heal this defect, mend the wound, perfect the imperfect. In my case, as my mother was no longer around, I think I was hoping the father would be part of the healing process.

Years went by and the frustration and torment of not knowing my ancestry were inescapable. Hence my next efforts to establish paternity. At around that time, I vividly recall the feeling of being in no man's land. Caught somewhere between what I had become and what I could have been. Being wanted by my adoptive parents and being labelled "the special one" didn't cut it anymore and hadn't for many years. Being "the special one" didn't compare to being unwanted by my birth mother. I didn't feel chosen; I felt rejected. I asked myself what I had done as a tiny baby to become unchosen and rejected. My mother wouldn't have given away a good baby, surely? Therefore, I must have been a dreadful baby.

Since the abandonment occurred so early in my life, as for many adoptees, I wasn't given the tools to cope, and therefore I just had to cope in whatever way I could. My behaviour as a child and growing

Playing on the beach on a sunny day. The bandages on my arms were to help protect me from the sun!

up manifested in different ways, which I am at last beginning to understand. For example, I have vivid memories of standing in the school playground at Infant School, sobbing that nobody loved me or was interested in playing with me.

The fear of being unworthy has probably caused more trouble in my life than most other things. I have always been very sensitive to criticism or the slightest hint of rejection, and I am at a loss to know how it can stop being triggered. When this happened as a younger person, I used to retreat into myself, felt worthless and basically agreed with what was being said. As an adult, I have noticed this reaction when in the company of people who are articulate. Nothing intimidates me more than articulate people. They always make me feel small and pathetic. It's not their problem; it's mine. Still, to this day, I tend to clam up when I'm in the company of "intellectuals". I try to handle things differently these days. I fight back more and defend my corner. I mentally "big myself up" on what I have achieved over the years, particularly from the age of 25 onwards. I see criticism as a challenge to tackle head-on, but only if I see the need, which isn't always. At the grand old age of 53, I feel I'm winning the battle against the fear of feeling unworthy.

The need to stave off more rejection and loss has always been top of my priority list for obvious reasons. The energy I have needed to exert across the years to maintain this is unmeasurable. This has been managed by adopting learned behaviour such as "wanting to be liked" by those around me. Having special talents at football in my younger years was helpful in this case. Traits such as the ability to make my peers laugh have been helpful as I have grown older. It has taken a tremendous effort, though. The fear of rejection has diminished with age as I have learned to handle it better. For example, my ability to handle comments about my personal appearance is certainly more advanced than it used to be.

CHAPTER FOUR

Picking Up the Thread Again

It was 2014, and I was now in my mid-forties. I must have been going through a challenging time mentally, hence feeling the need to pick up the thread again. After a 12-year gap, I thought it was time to try again to make contact with those in the frame for fathering me. *Maybe they will be more receptive this time? Maybe they have mellowed? Maybe their conscience has been pricked and they want to do the right thing? For god's sake! What harm can it do? All I want to do is establish where I have come from; it's not too much to ask, is it? Surely, it's my human right to know this fundamental information?*

I was now living in a different county to when I last approached social services. The social services I approached were therefore based in a different local authority area. During my first meeting with my assigned social worker, I recounted my story and journey to date. The social worker listened with intent. She seemed interested in what I was saying, especially my rationale for undertaking the search. After I had described my journey to date, I noticed the conversation started to shift, from me to her. It turned out she was also adopted. What a coincidence. Strangely, I found myself listening to her story. Her story didn't have a happy ending. She became emotional, and I found myself consoling her. This wasn't how I envisaged the meeting would pan out. When she calmed down, she outlined her thoughts going forward. It wasn't what I expected. She said it wasn't good practice to revisit the work previously undertaken by another authority, especially when there had been a negative outcome. She wasn't willing to act in an intermediary capacity and encouraged me to abort the search. On reflection, I wasn't sure what the dominant factor in her decision was – organisational protocol or her personal experience of an adoption search. I left the meeting quite deflated. I thought these people were there to assist you. Had she thrown in the towel too easily? Or was it in my best interests not to pursue it? However you want to describe it, I took this as another knockback on this journey. The waves of inquisitiveness continued. My resilience was holding out. Just.

CHAPTER FIVE

The 2020 Challenge

It was 1 January 2020. When people make New Year's resolutions, it's generally linked to losing weight, undertaking more exercise or something along those lines. Mine wasn't exactly a New Year's resolution. It was more of a personal target I set myself. It was to nail this paternity search once and for all. The question was could I do it? Up until this point, my ongoing adoption search had been a private matter. I had pretty much kept it to myself, apart from certain family members having some knowledge of it.

My wife had been my only support throughout each stage to date. This changed in December 2019 when I recruited an accomplice! He was an addition to the team and could be trusted. This wasn't done deliberately. It was an offer made out of kindness after we had talked about it on a night out. I appreciated the help. He was there as a support every step of the way, along with my wife, elder daughter and brother-in-law.

My search efforts to date had involved turning to professional bodies such as Social Services. Despite their best intentions, these had failed. It was time to try something different. My accomplice and I started plotting and hatched a plan. The plan was to focus on one of the individuals in my adoption paperwork and encourage him to take a DNA test. Sounds easy, doesn't it, when you say it out loud? We chose the individual who had been the more cooperative when approached by Social Services back in 2002. He was also considered the rank outsider of the two. The idea was that this approach would rule him out. Through our research, we established this individual had run a business and it was likely he was now retired. The website for the business included a mobile phone number for his son. My accomplice made contact via a text message, under the pretext of supporting a friend who was undertaking research on his family tree. This "white lie" was enough to open the door for me to start a dialogue, but soon we had to spill the beans and inform him of the real reason for making contact. We knew we were being disingenuous, but we needed a way in. Luckily, this didn't spook him, and he was quite receptive. In fact, he knew some sketchy details about his father being interviewed in 1968 in relation to the pregnancy of a local girl, and he agreed to help. What a relief. A result, in my eyes. Following several conversations with him, a decent relationship was forming. He definitely wanted to assist. He didn't inform his father, though, whom he was trying to keep at arm's length from this search. I didn't push it. Something even came to light from one of our conversations. It was his mother, rather than his father, who had spoken to Social Services in 2002. She was the one who had responded to the letter and showed empathy towards my situation. She turned out to be a rock and a wonderful support for the remainder of my journey. At last, I felt some progress was being made.

CHAPTER SIX

DNA Testing – Take One

He (the son) agreed to a DNA test. The selected DNA testing company was called Cellmark, which is an accredited testing laboratory approved by Government. Cellmark confirmed that a test with a half-sibling (as could be the case) might be less conclusive than if the test was with my potential biological father. However, what it could show was that we had the same Y chromosome. This is the Y-STR profile unchanged from father to son, and therefore all males in a family through the male line share the same Y-STR profile. This was a chance I had to take.

It was now July 2020. The first lockdown, as a result of the COVID -19 pandemic, had slowed things down somewhat. I realised, through talking to representatives at Cellmark, that there were different options in collecting DNA samples and it didn't need to be through using their collection service. It was possible to purchase home testing kits, and this was also a cheaper option. I realised this came with risks. How could I be 100 per cent sure the other person would undertake the test properly or that it was, in fact, them who undertook the test before sending it back to be analysed? I trusted the person I was dealing with. I had become friends with him on Facebook, and also with his mum. At one point, his mum had said, "If it is a positive test, we'll welcome you into our family with open arms." Although this was an amazing gesture, it was also scary. I wasn't going through this process to find a new family; far from it. It gave me a warm feeling, though. The one thing that wasn't clear was whether the father of the family was aware of what was going on. He was described as "old school", so I could understand the rationale for his being in the dark. I was just pleased the test had been agreed to. The question was would the test throw up a conclusive result?

It was towards the end of July when my test kit arrived. I was hoping this was going to be the best £99.99 I'd ever spent. It was a swab test. Very simple and quick to administer. You were just required to rub the swab on the inside of the cheeks for 10 seconds, then press the swab firmly onto the pink section of a labelled collection card for 5 seconds. I undertook the test and forwarded it to the individual I was to be tested against. I was relying on him to do the business now. I waited nervously. Approximately a week later, I received the DNA test report via email. I felt sick. I cautiously opened the email, followed by the report document. I skimmed the blurb quickly to get down to the nitty-gritty, the results. The result was spelled out in bold text. There was NO RELATIONSHIP between me and the individual I had been tested against. Pent up emotion going back years rose to the surface. I cried. Stopped and cried again. Had I just narrowed down the field to one runner? Did that mean the other individual was my biological father? He had always been the front runner, based on the photographs I was given by my biological grandmother. I relayed the news to my wife, close family and accomplice. This news didn't surprise them.

The individual who I was tested against was informed of the result, as was his mother. I explained that I had inherited a different Y marker, which indicated we did not share the same male lineage. There was a tinge of disappointment their side. Maybe they had geared themselves up to welcoming in a new family member. I thanked them for their support and we promised to keep in touch, and that has been the case ever since.

CHAPTER SEVEN

One Down, One to Go

The way forward sounded simple as it rolled off the tongue. "One down, one to go." I knew that persuading the second individual named in the adoption papers to undertake a DNA test would be a completely different proposition. Sadly, I had formed a view of this individual and it wasn't positive. Rightly or wrongly, I'd formed this belief without having met him (we can't count the time I stood next to him whilst waiting for the bomb squad to disperse the device in Manchester city centre) or giving him the opportunity to give his account of the story. My view was based on statements recorded in the official adoption paperwork from 1968. Statements such as *"I will never accept this child as mine"*, coupled with his attitude and offensive behaviour in court when interviewed and disclaiming any interest in the baby's future. Unfortunately, this stance was lodged in my memory bank. Wanting to keep his freedom for much longer but remain in an intimate relationship with the mother of the child was another comment he made. In other words, in my view, he was interested in the sex, but not the commitment. I also wasn't impressed by his reaction to the social worker when contacted in 2002. I thought he was selfish, spineless and lacking in responsibility. I hated him with a vengeance. Was I right or was I wrong to form these views? I was hoping time would tell. I knew that this next stage of the search was going to be challenging.

I drafted him a letter. It was to the point. It included the following: an explanation of who I was; an explanation of who my biological mother was; a reminder that he was interviewed in 1968 in relation to the pregnancy of a local girl, along with another individual; that this other individual had recently taken a DNA test (well, his son had) and the test was negative. Towards the end of the letter, I encouraged him to make contact. I ended the letter by stating that if he didn't respond, I would understand and that I wouldn't contact him again. I gave him a two-week window to get in touch with me. I sent it first class and hoped for the best.

As anticipated, no response came. No emails. No letter. No phone call. No text message. Nothing. What now? The natural reaction would have been to back off. F**k that! I had another plan. I was going to see him. I put pen to paper again. Within the letter, I included the date of my proposed visit. Whereas last time there had just been silence, suddenly my mobile phone started ringing and voice messages were left. His voice message indicated that he would be away for the weekend the day I planned to pay him a visit. A likely story! Via text message, we organised to have a chat a couple of days later.

1 September 2020. The arranged telephone call wasn't until 6.30 that evening. I had a full day's work ahead of me. Nerves kicked in shortly before the call. In my mind, I was about to speak to someone who could be my biological father for the first time in my life. I rang his number. Although my letters had been on the aggressive side (well, the second letter was, anyway), I didn't approach the telephone conversation in the same manner. I didn't let my frustration show, or my hatred of him.

The conversation didn't go according to plan. We seemed to talk more about him: his health; the impact of COVID; the state of his property; his deceased wife. We covered it all. He started crying. Just as in the meeting with the social worker in 2014, I found myself in some sort of counselling role. I wasn't expecting this. I wanted to talk about 1967/8, his involvement with my mother, his memories of that time, key dates and so forth. He was vague, the information was sketchy and I didn't learn anything new. He knew where I was trying to lead him (towards a DNA test), but he kept blocking me. His response was: "I can't help you." This phrase was repeated at least half a dozen times during the conversation. I was losing the battle, and as every second passed, I was running out of things to say. With gritted teeth, I ended the call. I remained calm and friendly and explained that I was there for him if he ever wanted a chat, but I was deflated. That had been my chance to make some significant progress in this search. It didn't happen. I thought I might have blown it.

CHAPTER EIGHT

Going to Court

For the next few weeks, I pondered and tried to conjure up my next move, but I wasn't exactly sure there was one. I had seen something in the media about a case linked to "puberty-blocking drugs" for children with gender dysphoria. The kids had won their case under the human rights agenda. This triggered something in me. I asked myself whether my search needed to go in a new direction and what the rights of an adult child were to identify their parentage. I soon realised there was lots of material on the internet on this subject, including examples of cases where individuals were attempting to establish paternity through court proceedings.

Although my research took me down many cul-de-sacs, one link didn't. It led me to a document I wasn't aware of called a *C63 Form – Application for declaration of parentage under section 55A of the Family Law Act 1986.* Nobody had mentioned this to me before. Could this help? After reading it, it seemed to support what I was trying to achieve, and I was eager to steer the search in this direction. Completing the form was pretty straightforward. Understanding where to send it wasn't. Eventually, I was provided with the relevant forwarding email address and told the location of the family court was in a nearby town. An application fee of £365.00 was required to accompany the form. This fee wasn't taken lightly. Costs linked to this search were beginning to stack up, and we were not particularly well off. I was conscious of that.

Within a week, an official-looking letter arrived from the court acknowledging receipt of my application and requesting that I complete a witness statement and return it by a given date. To my surprise, it looked as if the application was being taken seriously. My confidence was beginning to grow. I was liking this new search direction. The witness statement requested information such as why I believed the respondent (the individual listed in the adoption paperwork) might be my father, the reasons for establishing paternity and the steps I had taken to resolve this without proceedings. I felt the witness statement I drafted was strong. It had to be if I was to get into a courtroom. I submitted the following response and waited.

Witness Statement:
Re: S55 FLA 1986 – Declaration of Parentage
Case No – XT31R22214
Applicant: Peter Darren Jackson
Respondent: Derek James Forsyth

....

a) Why he believes that the Respondent may be his father

The applicant was adopted in 1968. The name of the applicant's father is not stated on his birth certificate. Two males were interviewed by the Area Children's Officer for Rochdale, Greater Manchester, in May/June 1968 in respect to being father of the applicant, and both of these individuals are named in the adoption documentation. One of these individuals is the Respondent [Mr Derek James Forsyth], who was stated as being in a relationship with the applicant's mother for two years when she fell pregnant. The Respondent has always denied being father of the applicant, but this has never been proved or disproved. Other indications supporting a link between the applicant and the Respondent are they have a similar build and skin tone. Photographic evidence attached to this application demonstrates a strong likeness between the two.

The second individual interviewed in 1968 was George Robson. A DNA test was taken in July 2020 between the applicant and a first-degree relative (the son) of George Robson. The company responsible for the DNA analysis was Cellmark, which is on the accredited list for court-directed paternity testing. A DNA Relationship Analysis Report confirmed that there was no relationship between the applicant and this individual.

Based on the above information, the Respondent is strongly considered to be the father of the applicant, unless this can be disproved through a DNA test. Therefore, a test is sought.

b) How he has obtained the address and contact details of the Respondent

The address and contact details have been obtained through personal research undertaken by the applicant. The use of electoral records was useful in this process. The Respondent's name, age and address were listed on the adoption documentation in 1968 and this was used as a starting point for the search.

c) What information he has (including contact details) about his birth mother and whether he has or has had any contact with her, in particular about this application

The applicant's birth mother passed away in 1970 (death certificate available upon request) when the applicant was two years old. Due to this, the applicant has not had any contact with her. The applicant did meet the birth mother's parents on a number of occasions prior to their passing away. They provided the applicant with some personal items, including photos and keepsakes.

d) The reasons why he wishes to establish paternity

The applicant feels it is his basic human right to understand his heritage and know the name of his biological father. To date (for 52 years), this has been denied him. Not having this information has frustrated the applicant and affected his mental health and wellbeing over a long period. The applicant has his own family and wants to be in a position whereby he can provide accurate information in relation to their true ancestry. Understanding this information will bring closure to a difficult situation and give him peace of mind.

The applicant does not want a relationship with the Respondent, whatever the outcome of this case.

e) What steps he has made to try to resolve this without proceedings

Several efforts have been made to resolve this without proceedings, but no progress has been made.

In April 2002, the Respondent was contacted by Shirley McQueen, Social Worker for the Social Services Directorate at Lancashire County Council. This initial request was made to enquire whether the Respondent was willing to meet the applicant. This request was turned down immediately.

No further contact was made with the Respondent until 2020. During August 2020, two letters were sent to the Respondent encouraging him to make contact and begin an amicable dialogue about the situation. The first letter was ignored. Following the second letter, the Respondent agreed to communicate with the applicant via telephone call. This telephone call took place on Tuesday, 1 September 2020. During the conversation, the Respondent was asked whether he would agree to a face-to-face meeting and also a DNA test. The Respondent stated he did not want to meet the applicant, nor have a DNA test, and could not help him further. A final attempt prior to making this application was made to resolve this issue but was subsequently ignored.

f) Who he proposes undertakes the test and the cost of the testing

I propose that a test is undertaken between Mr Derek Forsyth (the Respondent) and Peter Darren Jackson (the Applicant). The cost of the test will be £150.00 if using an accredited company such as Cellmark.

g) Confirmation that he is able and willing to pay for the test

The applicant (Peter Darren Jackson) is willing to pay for the test.

I believe that the facts stated in this witness statement are true.

Signed: **Peter Jackson**
Date: **15 December 2020**

About three weeks later, a second official letter arrived from the court. On opening the letter, I discovered that I was being invited to a direction hearing later that month. The witness statement I filed must have been strong enough to trigger this. The courtroom beckoned, or it would have done but for COVID. The process was to take place via a remote hearing. The court would now have to serve the application, including my witness statement, to the respondent. For the very first time in the search, I felt I might have the upper hand. It wasn't me on the ropes anymore; it was him. Based on our recent chat, I knew this would not be what he wanted. I recall him saying, "I just want the whole thing to go away." Well, I wasn't going anywhere. The net was closing in, or so I thought.

The date of the court hearing arrived. It was 27 November 2020. This was to be a new experience for me. I was very anxious. The hearing was planned for 11.30 am but was delayed, not commencing until 12.15 pm. The judge called me first. He went on to introduce himself, confirmed who I was and explained the background to the reason for the hearing. This was delivered using a lot of legal jargon, but I got the gist. Then he proceeded to tell me he was about to call the respondent to join the conference call. I thought, *you'll be lucky, pal. There is no way he will pick up the phone.* Apparently, the respondent hadn't even confirmed his attendance with the courts. The judge rang the number three times and then called it a day. He explained to me that there could be all sorts of reasons why he hadn't picked the phone up and that sometimes the court experienced technical or connection problems. *This no show and disregard of the process will go against him,* I thought. But the judge seemed to take all this in his stride as if it happened on a regular basis. This annoyed me as I had followed the instructions in the paperwork to the letter.

With just two of us on the call, we weren't able to continue. The judge did, however, do some probing, which rattled me. He said he had read the evidence file and commented that he very rarely dealt with cases so historic. He was concerned I didn't have enough evidence and asked whether I had engaged the services of a solicitor. He also confirmed that he didn't have the power to compel an adult to give a DNA sample to establish paternity. I didn't know what to expect, but I wasn't expecting this response. I was hoping for a bit of sympathy, but that never came. His comments created a reaction from me; there was a paradoxical feeling that I was a victim in all this, and not for the first time, either. I was looking for someone to blame. Was this linked to the actual experience I was having in court or to a feeling of helplessness and undifferentiated anger about having been so manipulated due to being adopted? The severing of the tie to my birth mother and my biological roots often leaves me with a permanent feeling of being at the mercy of others. The fact that I cannot consciously remember the experience makes the impact even more devastating and perplexing.

I was fuming with the judge, and I let my frustration show. I wasn't anxious anymore, as at the start of the proceeding, and forgot who I was talking to. I pummelled away at the judge, explaining that here was the opportunity to establish whether the respondent was my natural birth father as other avenues had been explored and ruled out. This was the final piece of the jigsaw, as far as I was concerned, so let's get on with it. I didn't give him the respect he deserved. He wasn't impressed with me but agreed that a further hearing was required and said he would identify a future date. Before ending the call, due to my behaviour, he questioned whether I would prefer a different judge. I'd calmed down by this stage and said no, I was ok to go with him.

Before the court hearing, I had been in a confident frame of mind, feeling that the odds were weighted in my favour. I wasn't so sure now. Midway through December, the court served the paperwork for the next hearing. It was scheduled for 13 January 2021. This was to give the respondent a further opportunity to attend, and I wondered how he [Derek Forsyth] would feel. How would he react to receiving the paperwork from the courts for a second time? He couldn't hide for ever. The week before Christmas, I noticed a missed call on my mobile. On checking the number, I realised it was him, the respondent. I ignored it. I was engaged in a court process so thought it best not to make contact and allow this process to unfold.

CHAPTER NINE

Hitting Rock Bottom

The emotional effect and frustration of the search were taking their toll. It had been a long journey, going back years, with the last 12 months being particularly intense. The ups and downs of the search and the fact that there wasn't a well-trodden path to follow made it incredibly taxing. I thought I could cope, though. I was invincible, wasn't I? Then, on the Sunday before Christmas, I was out on my early morning walk in the town where I lived when suddenly, on the return leg of the walk, I started sobbing. I couldn't stop. I was plugged into the radio through my mobile at the time. Christmas Lights by Coldplay was playing. This didn't help. I carried on sobbing as I walked home. Luckily, I didn't pass any walkers and have to explain myself. Later that morning, as I was waiting for my wife outside a supermarket, I burst into tears again. This was getting embarrassing. I realised at this point I wasn't invincible. I had cracked, the search had consumed me and I was a mess.

The next couple of days were a struggle. I couldn't stop thinking about the interchange I'd had with the judge. He had asked whether I had sought advice from a solicitor. I hadn't, and this bothered me. The potential cost of this advice was putting me off. But what if the respondent had sought legal advice? Where would that leave me on

On the swings at the local playground. I think I was distracted by some of the other children who were also playing.

13 January? Could a lack of legal advice hinder the search for my natural parent? Was this becoming more of a financial issue than a human rights issue? Was this right? It felt like another hurdle to overcome and just added to my frustration. My accomplice made me aware that some solicitors offer a free initial consultation session to assess a case, and this was the direction I felt I needed to go in. I needed a solicitor who specialised in Family Law.

The first solicitors I contacted were local and in a nearby town, and although they called themselves a Family Law Centre, they confirmed they didn't have the expertise in their team to help me. I required someone who knew their way around paternity issues and DNA testing. The second solicitor I contacted seemed a good fit according to the blurb on their website. They were not local; they were Manchester-based. I dropped a message into their enquiry box, and within minutes, I received a telephone call from one of their lawyers. She confirmed she was willing to spend a few minutes assessing the case and that anything after that would be £200.00 per hour. She quickly got to grips with what I was looking to achieve and asked me a series of questions – questions I couldn't answer. It was like being in a courtroom. She bamboozled me. She explained at the start that she would be blunt and to the point, and she was true to her word. She finished the conversation by saying she wasn't sure whether the respondent was legally obliged to attend a court hearing and that the court didn't have the power to compel an adult to give a DNA sample to establish paternity. She promised to send through some information once she had made some enquiries. I put the phone down and stared out of the window. I was at rock bottom. What was the point of carrying on? I seemed to be wasting my time. I seemed to be wasting everybody's time. I had lost hope. This wasn't going to be a good Christmas. My wife was worried about my mental state and overall demeanour. The information promised by the lawyer never materialised.

CHAPTER TEN

DNA Test – Take Two

I contemplated the options available to me. One of them was to return the respondent's telephone call from a week ago. I had previously discounted this to focus on the court hearing, but now it was back on the table. My wife even offered to ring him, she was so frustrated. She was pushing for this, and she wanted to give him a piece of her mind after what she had seen I was going through. Like me, she couldn't understand why he was digging his heels in. Undertaking the DNA test wouldn't change his life whatsoever. I didn't want anything from him. It was about me understanding my biological heritage and helping me bring closure to an ongoing situation. It was the night before Christmas Eve. I sent him a text message. ME: *You left me a voicemail a few days ago. What do you want to chat about?* HIM: *Hello, I was hoping we could come to some agreement.* ME: *What sort of agreement are you proposing?* HIM: *One that would include a DNA test.* ME: *Ok, let's chat further. I'll give you a call tomorrow morning.* This was a massive breakthrough. I went to bed with hope.

It was Christmas Eve and I woke up early. My first task that morning was to pick up the Christmas turkey from the butcher's in town. After that, I made the call as promised. He explained to me that he had received some paperwork from the court and wasn't over-keen on going through a legal process. He went on to say he would consider having a DNA test but had a couple of questions first. This didn't worry me as this was major progress as far as I was concerned. The first question was linked to the pandemic. Since March, he had kept himself to himself, been extra cautious and not really interacted with family and friends. I explained that it was still possible to undertake the test and that we just needed to take precautions and stay two metres apart. I said we could undertake the test in his garden as I knew he didn't want me in his house. He seemed ok with my answer. Onto the next question. This was even easier to answer than the first. He explained he had a brother and two sisters and they were in line to inherit his estate in the future. I was curious where this question was leading. He said "if his inheritance could be protected", he would be happy to take the test. I couldn't believe what I was hearing. We were looking at this through different filters. He thought I was after his money. He had resisted making contact with me for all these years and now I knew why. I put these thoughts to one side and tried to reassure him. I was no expert on the subject, but I explained that my understanding was that, if an adoption is formalised under UK law, the legal relationship between the child and biological parent is severed and the child loses the legal right to inherit from their biological parents. He seemed to accept my answer. I reiterated that this wasn't about money for me, and never had been. He accepted this and agreed to take the test. At last, I had made a breakthrough. I wasn't 100 per cent there, but I was on my way. This could be the best Christmas present I'd ever had.

I wasted no time and ordered a home testing kit the day after Boxing Day. It arrived a couple of days later. This DNA test wasn't to be sent through the post like the first one. I wanted to be there in person. I insisted on this, as I wasn't entirely sure I could trust him. We agreed to meet on 2 January 2021 at 1.00 pm in a supermarket car park on the outskirts of Rochdale. This wasn't the ideal place to undertake a DNA test, but I wasn't complaining. Everything was in place and the day soon arrived.

I arrived at the car park safely and in good time. The trip down the M6 had flown by. It was a crazy situation. How had it come to this? Driving 125 miles with a DNA test kit in the boot of the car to meet a man I had never met before. It had been a traumatic journey to get to this point, but I had made it. I just had to pray he would show up.

During adolescence, when I was searching for my own identity without having that biological history to draw upon, I used to imagine what my birth parents, especially my father, would look like. I thought my father would resemble someone like Lee Majors (aka The Six Million Dollar Man). Some forty-odd years later, I was seconds away from potentially finding out.

As agreed, I rang him upon arrival at the supermarket car park. He confirmed he would be there in ten minutes, wearing a black coat, black trousers and dark glasses. He explained the dark glasses were worn due to an eye condition. I lifted the boot of my car, laid out the DNA test kit and waited. I could feel my heart racing. Was I about to meet my biological father for the first time in 52 years? How was I going to react? The hatred I had previously felt towards him had dissipated. Suddenly, there was a figure walking in my direction from the other side of the car park. It seemed to fit the description he had given me. Thinking back to my childhood, it didn't resemble Lee Majors though! I walked towards him. The moment was dreamlike. We shook hands. Not only was he wearing dark glasses; he was also wearing a hat. It was him alright. An older version of the man with my mother in the photograph. I thanked him for coming and for agreeing to take the test. He was pleasant towards me, apologising for making things difficult for me for all those years. I brushed it off as if it didn't matter, just wanting to get on with the test as my dread was that he would change his mind. I talked him through the process, and to his credit, he had taken on board my instructions about not eating 30 minutes before the test. He had even rinsed his mouth out with water. It only took a few seconds to complete, label and package up. I was dancing inside. I'd done it, achieved the impossible! I relaxed immediately. We stood and talked.

I was consumed by his appearance. Although he was in his mid-seventies, he seemed to have looked after himself. His teeth and fingernails were in good condition. His clothing was outdoor branded, high-end stuff. I didn't get the impression he relied on food banks. We were relaxed in each other's company. He told me about his hobbies. I talked about my family. There seemed to be a mutual respect, even an emotional connection. He apologised again, then he cried. I tried to steer the conversation in a different direction, telling him that I would be in touch as soon as the test results were in. We shook hands again. Then he turned and left. I drove out of the car park convinced I had just met my biological father. I felt wonderful.

I don't recall much of the drive home. When I arrived home, I put the DNA package in the post. Job done; I could do no more. For the next few days, I replayed the experience in my mind because it was so weird. On top of that, I was considering what the future might look like should this test be positive. Could there be a harmonious relationship with this man going forward? Would he want this? It was difficult to say.

Within a few days, the test results were back. I opened up the report. This was to be a momentous occasion for me that could bring closure to a quandary that had haunted me for years. In black and white, the report spelled out "This individual IS NOT your biological father." I couldn't believe it. I went quiet. How could this be? Had there been a mistake in the testing process? Human error? Surely not? This was an accredited company I was using. In the photos I have, we even look alike. Both parties listed in my adoption paperwork had been tested, and both had come out negative. This was supposed to be a two-horse race. There must have been another party involved, someone who wasn't interviewed at the time. The outcome I had anticipated had not borne fruit, and more importantly, the conclusion I was hoping to reach, that is, identifying my biological father, had not been achieved. I was shattered. Pretty devastated, really.

CHAPTER ELEVEN

DNA Test – Take Three

I reflected for a few days on the information I had received. I read the report again. Had I dotted all the i's and crossed the t's? There was one avenue I hadn't explored. For the first test, I had agreed to undertake the DNA test with the son of the individual named in the adoption papers because I was conscious of not wanting to rock the boat. I knew it was a sensitive subject and I was just relieved that this family were willing to help. A test directly with the individual himself would have been the preferred course of action, but this didn't happen as I hadn't pushed for this. After consideration, I decided to contact Cellmark. My question to them was as follows: if a DNA test was undertaken with a potential biological father, rather than his son, could this change the outcome of the test? Cellmark responded by saying yes, this was possible. However, the first test had picked up that I had inherited a different Y marker to the individual I was tested against, which indicated that we did not share the same male lineage. A test result may be different in the unlikely event that mutation had taken place. Decision made. I had to have this final DNA test and feel confident that I had done everything in my power as part of the search. Otherwise, it would play on my mind for the rest of my life.

In the meantime, I had forwarded a copy of the DNA test results to the individual I met in the supermarket car park, as promised. Shortly after he had received the results, we spoke on the telephone. He was empathetic towards me and disappointed that I hadn't resolved the situation, confirming that he thought he was "in the frame" to be my father. Although he didn't say it, I sensed a tinge of disappointment, but that is only an opinion I formed during that short exchange. We did, however, agree to remain in touch with each other, which was really positive.

The next task was to go back to the family who had assisted with the first test. The challenge was to encourage the father to follow in the footsteps of his son and take the test. I had remained in touch with the mother of the family via social media, so she wasn't surprised when I got in touch. Within ten minutes of making the request, she dropped me a line back saying they wanted to help out all they could, and so the answer was yes, her husband was willing to take the test. I was so relieved. Another test was ordered straight away. I was used to the process by now. The staff at Cellmark were pretty familiar with me, too. Within a few days, both of us had undertaken the test and it was back at Cellmark to be analysed. Deep down, I think I knew what the outcome of the test would be, but a small part of my brain was saying *you never know*. This whole journey had been full of twists and turns, so there could be one more twist. Upon receiving the report, I scrolled down to the bottom, and it once again spelled out "This individual IS NOT your biological father." I sat down quietly. I looked at my wife. She knew the outcome of the result by the look on my face. I knew the search was now over. But I still didn't know who my biological father was.

CHAPTER TWELVE

Sourcing the Inquest Report

Although I'd exhausted the obvious lines of enquiry, my brother-in-law suggested that I should try and source my mother's Inquest Report, just in case it highlighted anything I wasn't aware of that could assist my search. On the face of it, this document shouldn't have been particularly difficult to get hold of. As with the rest of this search, this wasn't the case, and there were more challenges to overcome. Initially, I was told by the Coroner's Administrator, who was assisting me track down the records, that due to the records dating back to 1970, they would be held in the City Hall Archives in Manchester. A few weeks into the search, I was informed by the administrator that she had received correspondence from staff at the City Hall Archives stating that as the records dated before 1974, they would not be held with the collective records in that building. Staff at the City Hall Archives suggested she try the local archives closest to the town where I was born. However, they also informed her this building was currently closed due to refurbishment and they were unsure whether the records would be held there or somewhere off-site. Due to a combination of building refurbishments and COVID-19 restrictions, I was informed the earliest the records could be located was July 2021 and was asked whether this was acceptable. I felt I didn't have much choice so went along with it.

Since requesting the inquest report, things had played on my mind. What if there was a nugget of information buried within this transcript that could assist with the search to find my biological father? Also, should I have requested this information much sooner on this journey? In line with their predicted July timeline, the Coroner's Administrator emailed all the inquest report records across to me on 7 July 2021, with the attached message: "Please note that most of these records are handwritten and not necessarily the easiest to read."

What I hadn't stopped to fully consider was what I was about to read, which was essentially a record of the last 24 hours of my biological mother's life! I perhaps should have thought about this beforehand and realised that the information would more than likely be very upsetting. As I began to work my way through the data in front of me, I became absorbed in the detail. My overall aim of identifying a lead for the ongoing search was superseded as I became engrossed in the events that unfolded on Sunday, 14 June 1970. It wasn't a pleasant read. An extract taken from the transcript had been provided by her father and read as follows:

"I live at 196 Mayo Lane, Littleborough, Greater Manchester, and I am a coal worker. Glenda Alice Curruthers was my daughter. She was 26 years of age, born 1st April 1944 and also living at 196 Mayo Lane. She was a typist and a spinster and was in the care of Dr Lucas. When she was about 4 years of age she was found to be suffering from a mild form of epilepsy, but was otherwise healthy and active. She was receiving treatment for the epilepsy in the form of phenobarbitone and mycilin. About two years ago she was a patient at Rochdale Hospital after an overdose of tablets. She was in hospital about four weeks.

On Sunday 14th June 1970, at about 12.30am, I was at home when my daughter came home. She told me that she had had an argument with her boyfriend, Derek Forsyth. She went to bed at about 3.30am and seemed depressed. She stayed in bed most of that day and refused to eat. At about 7.30pm, I was at home, and I heard her talking to her mother in her bedroom. At about 9.10pm, I left home for work and at 9.40pm, as a result of something said to me by Trevor Fernsby (a fellow coalminer), I returned home. My wife told me that my daughter had telephoned Mrs Rita Fernsby [wife of Trevor] from home and had told her that she had taken an overdose. Mrs Fernsby had ordered an ambulance and then informed my wife. When the ambulance came my daughter was taken in it to Rochdale Hospital. Before being admitted, she told Mrs Fernsby that she had taken a number of tablets."

Glenda eventually passed away on 29 June 1970, at 5.25 am, as a result of the overdose. I was consumed by sadness. I had never considered the events leading up to the suicide. What turmoil she must have been going through and how helpless she must have felt as she swallowed pill after pill on that Sunday evening. We will never be able to measure the extent of her instability at that time. The state of her mental health must have been off the scale. Giving up your baby must be one of the hardest things a woman can do. Yet we have established through the Inquest Report that this wasn't the first time an overdose had been attempted. Although dates aren't provided, the timeline suggests that an overdose was taken soon after I was born and given up.

Glenda had obviously reached the point of desperation. Whether she was physiologically, emotionally and spiritually ready to welcome me into the world and bond with me, I'll never know. What I do know is that she never had the chance to do so. She was left with the feeling of waiting for something to happen that never did. She experienced the black hole of despair, instead of the pure white light of union with her child. It is interesting to understand that when Glenda was at crisis point and consumed 50 tablets, washed down with a bottle of pop, she didn't turn to her mother for help but, instead, phoned a friend, who went on to phone for an ambulance. This perhaps could begin to tell us the state of the relationship between Glenda and her mother leading up to her suicide.

CHAPTER THIRTEEN

Introducing Social Media

I must be one of those people who don't know when to quit. Who could I ask who might know something about the events in 1968 which led to my biological mother's pregnancy? Was there someone out there who could help me generate a new lead in terms of who the potential father was? With this in mind, I started searching Facebook groups. This wasn't an avenue I had explored previously as social media hadn't been created when I first started out on my search journey. As I was investigating an event from the past, I felt I needed to contact a Facebook group whose emphasis was on times gone by. I wasn't too long into my search when I came across a Facebook group called Littleborough People – Past & Present. I wondered whether my enquiry would fit with the ethos of this group and whether the Administration would block it. I didn't think I had anything to lose and posted a photo of my biological mother, explaining she had passed away in 1970 and I was researching my family tree; any information linked to her would be useful. Fortunately, Admin didn't block it. The response to my request was astonishing.

Many people knew of the Curruthers family. Some messages were received from individuals whose parents lived in the same lane. Other messages came from people who had worked with her at some point in their careers. One person got in touch who, along with his family, had lived next door to her in 1968. There were also people whose older brothers and sisters knew of her, or who had been friends with her all those years ago. I also received messages from relatives, including cousins. One cousin explained she had been particularly close to my mother and had visited me as a newborn in hospital. It was lovely of her to communicate with me, bearing in mind she was being treated for cancer at the time. Her daughter even sent me a photograph of my mother as a bridesmaid at a family wedding.

It was obvious that the pregnancy was a well-guarded secret. I sent some direct messages to those who I thought might be able to provide a new lead. The responses to my questions were either rumours they had heard at the time or hearsay. Some people didn't even know she had given birth; they thought she'd had a miscarriage. Nobody could offer any significant information, especially about who the father might be. The general response was either it was a local lad or a colleague she worked with. This information was no good to me. It was a name I was after, or information about her place of work just before she came pregnant. This would have been more tangible. Although people were being as helpful as they could be, their information wasn't aiding my search.

A couple of weeks went by and incoming messages from this Facebook group began to dry up. As I had little else to go on, I did wonder whether there was any other Facebook group where I could post a similar message that might widen the search and prompt people to get in touch with me. A quick search showed there was. This time the group was called Rochdale Past and Present. A message was soon posted, and it didn't take long before members of this group were leaving me comments.

This time, it was mainly old friends of Glenda who contacted me. One old friend recalled Glenda going to her house when her own children were young. Once again, old neighbours who recalled the family got in touch. One neighbour recalled that he occasionally used to have a pint in a pub called the Red Lion with Glenda's dad. However, none of the people I contacted could add any further information. Key information such as who she socialised with or where she worked in the summer of 1967 simply was not forthcoming. However, the name of an employer (Whittles Bakery) kept cropping up, but nobody could be specific about dates when she worked there. Some people were aware she'd had a baby and it had been adopted. Most gave the impression she didn't really want to give the baby up. She was described as a quiet girl who may have suffered from mild learning difficulties.

CHAPTER FOURTEEN

3 Out of 6 Gone

A common message that occurred from my post to both Facebook groups was that Glenda had a brother called Gavin. I was well aware of this, having met him, his wife and their children back in 1994, soon after I turned up at 196 Mayo Lane unannounced. I had not been in touch with members of my new biological family since retrieving my adoption papers in 2002. Nor had they tried to make contact with me. Back then, Gavin was a well-respected Managing Director of a company, whilst I was a mature student attending College. He was friendly enough towards me, but I didn't sense he was overjoyed I had turned up at his parents' house out of the blue, searching for my mother. The question was could he hold the key to this mystery? After all, it was his sister who had been pregnant. Somebody had to ask the awkward questions all those years ago and try to sort things out. Maybe he took on that role. If anyone knew who my father was, maybe it was him, and he was keeping quiet. He'd never mentioned anything in the 90s, the few times I had spent time with him. If truth be told, though, I'd never asked him, either. In fact, I'd never asked anyone.

With a lack of leads to go on, I made the decision to try and contact Gavin. I tried LinkedIn first but without success. Facebook seemed the next-best option. Although I noticed he had a Facebook account, the last time he had posted anything was in 2012. This seemed a little strange. Due to this oddity, I thought I would try to track down his wife, Karen, to see if she had a Facebook account too. It might explain the lack of activity on Gavin's page. Her Facebook page was pretty much up to date. However, scrolling through it, I noted there were details of a life-changing event in 2012. Her husband Gavin had died. No details as to the circumstances of the death were provided, but it was clear she was now a widow.

This unexpected news was an eye-opener for me. Time was passing by more quickly than I thought. Three members of my biological family who had been there at the start of the search were now deceased. I began to question myself. Should I have stayed in touch with the family once I had accessed my adoption papers? Should I have been more lenient towards the family situation all those years ago? Perhaps if I hadn't let my emotions get the better of me and cut ties with them, I might have got to know them better. They might have helped me with the search, and I might have been able to resolve this years ago. But I'd gone down a different path, so I'll never know.

This news about Gavin certainly gave me food for thought. I couldn't waste any more time. Act now, not tomorrow was the phrase at the forefront of my mind. I decided to contact Gavin's wife. I wasn't sure how the message would be received, and I knew it had to be sensitive. The message was as follows:

"Hi Karen, I hope you don't mind me contacting you. We met several years ago (1994) when I started to look for my birth parents. I have recently resumed the search for my biological father and in doing so I now know that Gavin is deceased. I am very shocked and I would like to offer my condolences to you and your family."

36 hours after sending the message, I still hadn't received an acknowledgement. Maybe she was considering her response before replying. After all, I'd not been in touch for about 20 years. Worse still, maybe she wasn't going to get in touch at all. A further 24 hours passed and still nothing. Also, the green light that shows up when you are active on Messenger was never on when I checked. This wasn't looking too promising.

Just when I thought I would receive no further messages from the Facebook groups I had contacted, another message dropped in, and it was a stunner. Amazingly, it was from Karen's sister. Unbelievably, it said the following: "Hi, I understand you are asking for information on Glenda. I did know her, as her brother Gavin was my brother-in-law. Gavin died nine years ago. He was married to my sister, who tragically died suddenly, only last week." Was this really happening to me? Everyone I was trying to make contact with was no longer around.

Hearing about the passing of Gavin, and now Karen, was a reminder that we are not immortal, and this news touched a chord. Perhaps it was because I had been looking at her recent Facebook posts, but I couldn't imagine her moving from one world to another in such as short space of time. On my mind were a photo and a post from her Facebook account. It was a family wedding photo showing her with five other family members (including Gavin) and a poignant post saying "3 out of 6 gone". This post was stuck in my head for days.

Knowing this recent tragic news, combined with drawing a blank with recent requests for help through Facebook groups, I was deliberating my next move. Remarkably, though, I was still in a good place. There was a colossal difference in my mental well-being. Having the scientific clarification that neither of the two individuals named in the adoption papers was my biological father was a huge step forward. The frustration that had plagued me for years had now been released. Although it is a strange analogy, I can only compare it to "bleeding a radiator", where I had let out the anguish that had been trapped in my system for what seemed an eternity. To some extent, I now felt more in control of the search. Although I still hadn't found what I was looking for, I remained positive.

CHAPTER FIFTEEN

Research Company

One evening in February 2021, I was watching an episode of Long Lost Family when I noticed the focus was on a foundling's incredible journey to Hong Kong in search of information about her origins. A foundling is an infant that has been abandoned by its parents and is discovered and cared for by others. Her search was difficult for many reasons, and her parents weren't identified or found. However, this episode had a different conclusion to most of the others I had watched over the years. The foundling's DNA was input into several DNA search engines, and she was introduced to a number of individuals and their families where there was a shared DNA match, albeit not direct matches. This made me wonder whether this kind of service was available to me. After all, I'd tried everything else I could think of. I wasn't exactly sure where to find this type of support but thought an enquiry on the Long Lost Family website might be a good place to start.

I noticed on their website that a designated research company supported the programme. I sent a message enquiring whether they could support someone in my situation. Based on the chat room message that came back, it seemed they would be happy to help. Following this, a telephone conversation was arranged with a member of their team a few days later. During this call, I provided a short summary of my search to date and what I was trying to achieve. The person I spoke to seemed very genuine and confident that they would be able to help me progress in my search. He explained that their company had a 94% success rate in helping people trace family and relatives. He went on to explain their company used several databases that held the DNA of several million people. Providing a sample of my DNA would give them a foothold into the right family lines. So, for example, if I was matched with a third cousin or closer, they could then work back through the family history to build out a family tree using their genealogical expertise. It would be a four-stage process, and their team would support me and keep me updated every step of the way.

The information relayed to me was perfect. In fact, it was too good to be true. Why hadn't I found out about this research company sooner? It could have saved me so much heartache and frustration. Then came the sucker punch. The cost. Their service was too expensive for my budget. I ended the call, explaining I would need to think about it. I knew I didn't have nearly £3000 sitting idle. And even if I had, it would probably be better utilised on other things, such as a family holiday or home improvements. I deliberated over this for a few days. I once again questioned the ethics of the search. Was it being driven by my human right to fully understand my parentage? Or was it determined by finance and my ability to personally fund the search? What would happen if there were no further funds available? Could I rely on my human rights to continue this search? And if so, how much progress would I make? I came to the conclusion that my human rights had played little or no part in this search to understand my parentage. It was finance, along with my sheer determination and resilience, which had driven it forward. Finance to pay for court fees and finance to pay for DNA tests. This didn't seem right, though. If one was unable to finance such a search, what would be the outcome? To go through life not knowing one's biological parents. This thought just made me angry as it seemed so unjust. What could be done for people who find themselves in my position and don't have the financial means to undertake their search? That was a discussion for another day. I had to make a decision on whether I was going to use this research company or not, and if so, how I could finance it.

At around this time, there was a new three-part documentary showing on BBC 2 called DNA Family Secrets. It was about helping people find genetic answers using the power of DNA. After watching the first episode, I realised the process used on the programme was similar to that proposed by the research company with whom I had made enquiries. The programme provided real-life examples of tracing the families of people who were in exactly the same position as me. If I didn't take this next step, I would never know whether it could have worked for me, especially as I had come such a long way on my journey, particularly over the last 12 months or so. I discussed it with my wife. She'd anticipated I would want to proceed and said we'd somehow find the money to finance the search. A couple of days later, I confirmed with a member of staff at the research company that I was planning to proceed. The cost could be paid in four instalments, which made it more affordable, and I duly made my first payment, not knowing whether this was a good investment or not. I knew at the time that this was the start of the last leg of this journey. I was also oblivious as to how it would end.

It took approximately 10 days for the test kits to arrive, although it felt like twice that time, if I'm honest. The test kits were from companies called 23andme and Ancestry DNA. This time, I was required to fill a tube with saliva for the test, rather than provide a swab. I did both tests, packaged them up and mailed them back within 24 hours of receiving them. I sensed a sigh of relief after stepping away from the letter box. I knew that what happened from this point onwards was beyond my control. Up to now, the outcome of previous tests hadn't gone my way. Whilst waiting for the testing kits to arrive, my feelings about the whole thing were topsy turvy. Some days I would feel optimistic, whereas other days I would feel that I was destined never to know the outcome of this journey. For some reason, I had the odd day where I had morbid thoughts and felt that this was a race against time. That I would meet my maker before getting to the end of the search. I know these were stupid thoughts, but this is how the search was impacting me. I even mentioned to my wife, after making the first payment, that if something should happen to me, she should continue with the search in my absence and see it through.

After mailing my saliva samples back to both companies (23andMe and Ancestry DNA), it wasn't long before I started to receive progress updates via email. It soon became apparent that analysing DNA was a complex process. It was going to involve a series of chemical reactions, multiple cycles of heating and cooling and a lot of complicated equipment. I would need to be patient and allow the whole process to unfold.

The first stage was to extract my DNA. This meant freeing my DNA from the cheek, gum and white blood cells in my saliva and copying my DNA millions of times, before cutting it up into many pieces, cleaning it and measuring it. The second stage was about genotyping my DNA. Using technology, scientists are able to read around 600,000 letters in DNA, and then use probes to turn DNA samples into knowledge. The third stage was about reviewing my genetic data. Using powerful computers and software, scientists make sense of the raw data from the lab, including translating colours into DNA letters.

CHAPTER SIXTEEN

Ancestry DNA Results

The 23andMe DNA results were uploaded onto my account first. The results were fascinating. In addition to my ancestry composition and ancestral breakdown, which indicated likely origins of ethnicity and recent ancestor locations, a number of other reports were included. These specifically related to my traits and health. Although this was all important stuff, the priority for me was to understand whether my DNA linked me to any other relatives. When I opened the DNA relatives report, I was astounded. I shared DNA with 1500 other 23andMe customers. This included two second cousins once removed. One of these second cousins was called Jennifer Myers, who was based in Ontario, Canada. She was keen to share her family tree with me to see if it would help unlock my ancestral jigsaw. We were confident we shared the same set of great-grandparents. She shared this information and her own ancestral research with the team from the research company who were assisting me. I understand it backed up some of their research findings, and I will always be grateful to Jennifer for her assistance with this.

The Ancestry DNA results took slightly longer to be released but were equally fascinating. This revealed my ethnicity estimate was calculated as 39% England & north-western Europe, 30% Ireland,

16% Scotland, 12% Wales and 3% Norway. They revealed I shared DNA with hundreds more customers. To be precise, 469 fourth cousins or closer, including two first or second cousins. All this information and the ancestral connections were difficult to absorb.

My main point of contact with the research team supporting me was Gordon Ings. His role in the organisation was Trace Team Manager. Gordon contacted me intermittently between May and June 2021, mainly to provide updates in terms of the progress he was making. He was extremely efficient at his job and explained things in a user-friendly manner, so I could understand his methodology and reasoning. Towards the back end of Gordon's work, he explained he had narrowed down the search to two brothers, and he confirmed they were both still alive. This was astonishing news. I couldn't believe the swift progress being made since I had provided my DNA a matter of two months previously. I didn't press Gordon on any details as I knew he wouldn't be able to release them at this stage. I was just completely over the moon at what information had been established so far.

With the information backed up by genetic evidence, I was confident the appropriate individuals could be traced. For the first time, I also felt fully supported in this quest and that I wasn't on my own. I was experiencing a new feeling, as if my emotional frustrations linked to the search had now been passed across to somebody else to shoulder. My newfound friends in this research team had definitely become my comfort blanket and it was greatly appreciated. I realised there was an art to genealogy, and I placed my trust in Gordon to carry out this important piece of work. When asked, he confirmed to me that when his work was complete, and even if my biological father didn't respond to the correspondence they planned to send out, he would send me a full report which explained the investigation step by step. He would also transfer the paternal family tree across to my Ancestry account. This was something I could look forward to.

CHAPTER SEVENTEEN

Bureaucracy and Frustration

Once the research company trace team had concluded their exploration, my case was passed across to the Adoption Support team. Their role was to provide guidance and support to those involved in the search process. It was explained to me that this stage of the journey can be particularly emotional, and the outcomes can be unpredictable. The option of counselling was also offered as part of the support package, either now or further down the line, depending on how things went. My initial thought when I heard this was *surely this stage will be water off a duck's back, won't it, after all I have been through so far?* This opinion was formed without knowing what was ahead of me.

Prior to any discussions with the Adoption Team, they requested specific documentation from me to help them with their search. They needed to verify my identity and relationship to the subject. The following information was requested:

- Birth certificate – the original birth certificate stating my birth name
- Name of the adoption agency or local authority who had dealt with the adoption in 1968

- Adoption records
- Name of court/court order where the adoption order was granted
- Any relevant certificates and birth certificates demonstrating a clear record of any name change since birth (if this had been the case)

My initial consultation with a representative from the Adoption Team took place on 23 June 2021. It was designed to help me understand the process and for me to consider what some of the outcomes might be. It was explained that whilst their skilled team were able to trace my relatives, as they seem to have already done, they were not able to predict the outcome of the search nor have control over what might happen next. In their experience, the most common outcomes were as follows, and both positive and negative outcomes can be equally overwhelming.

- The person is found and is happy to have contact.
- The person is found and you find the relationship is more complex than you had anticipated.
- The person is found but does not want to have direct contact right now but will share information.
- The person is found but does not wish to have any contact under any circumstances.
- The person is found but has passed away.
- The person cannot be located.

The consultation was with a lady called Lydia. We got on really well and she put me at ease as we discussed what had been a long and difficult journey for me. Also, she genuinely seemed interested in the events I had faced over the last twenty years or so. Following this consultation, she emailed me a summarised record of the conversation. It read as follows:

Dear Peter,

Thank you for helping me to complete your initial consultation earlier today. I have attempted to capture as much of the information you shared as possible. If anything isn't quite right, please let me know and I will get it amended. You told me that you were adopted when you were approximately six months old and that you have been trying to trace your birth parents for over two decades. You gained access to your adoption records and initially traced your birth mother whom you discovered was deceased. After discovering this news, you decided to try to find your birth father. Unfortunately, you do not have a record of his identity.

After reading your adoption records and speaking with your maternal grandparents, you spent many years thinking that one of two men may have been your father. After quite some time you very recently had it confirmed that neither man is actually your father and you describe your disappointment at having been "chasing shadows" for so many years.

You came to the point of needing some help to find out who your birth father is and you are now ready to finally gain some closure.

Your Objective

Your best hope would be to have scientific evidence and a name that sits alongside it. Perhaps "the recognition that that person will see he has fathered somebody". You told me that you don't necessarily want a relationship with that person, if anything you only want the odd phone call or visit. You just want the answer that you have waited such a long time for. Effectively we concluded that you are looking for closure.

Your Action

You have sent in many documents to help in our search, thank you. If you could just send in the telephone number for your wife Katrina, that would be much appreciated as you have nominated her as your "Buddy".

Our Action

In the meanwhile, we will write to the Local Authority who were involved in your adoption in 1968, as it may be that they have some involvement in your case; we will await their response.

The next part of the search was for the Adoption Team to contact the Local Authority who dealt with the adoption originally. The Adoption Team were duty-bound by the regulations Ofsted set out to contact the adoption agency to check for any Vetoes/Do not Contacts when providing an intermediary service. There was a need to ask whether they had any relevant information with regard to the search and whether they had any views that needed to be taken into account when searching. It was made clear that this process could take four to six weeks for the Local Authority to check their records and respond.

Up until this point, the progress made by the research company supporting me had been rapid and far quicker than I could have imagined. This advancement of knowledge was impressive and filled me with hope that maybe I could reach a conclusion to this after all. However, this next stage was completely the opposite. Waiting for the Local Authority to respond was making me anxious. Over the last few weeks, I had been on a roll. I had gained some momentum with the search and I loved that feeling. But now I seemed to be at a standstill. I tried not to let it affect me, but the positive outlook developed as a result of a surge of progress was now being severely tested.

After what seemed an eternity, the period allocated for the Local Authority to respond lapsed. The Adoption Team reviewed my case and granted permission to proceed without a response. I was ecstatic. Game on. The next stage was for the research company to write to the person identified as the most likely to be my biological father based on the ancestral search undertaken by Trace Team Manager Gordon Ings. It was at this point I was asked to write a personal statement that provided a short explanation of who I was and why I was making contact. It was explained that this personal statement would be triggered if there was a response from the recipient to the letters forwarded by the research company. The personal statement read as follows:

Hello

My name is Peter, and I was adopted in 1968 when I was approximately six months old. I was told about my adoption when I was about 8 years old. Recently, I have been supported by an organisation who have assisted me as I attempt to trace my birth parents. I have always been naturally curious about my real identity. I know I was given up for adoption under difficult circumstances, but I am unaware of how much knowledge you have of this.

I am now 53. I am married with two daughters aged 18 and 12, and we live in the North of England. My eldest daughter has just completed her first year at University. I work in local government and my wife is a nurse.

I hope to find out some of my family history and would be pleased to meet you or any other family members. I understand that this may come as a shock and may take some getting used to. I do not want to intrude in your life; however, I would be happy just to have some information to let me have closure after such a long time wondering about my heritage. Please let me know if you would like contact. If not, I would be grateful if you could help with any health history that might be useful to me, by using an intermediary.

Kind regards
Peter

The Administrator at the research company supporting me clarified that my first letter had been posted on Wednesday, 1

September 2021. Once again, I was at the mercy of others as I waited for a response. I knew how I had reacted waiting for the Local Authority to respond, but this was even worse. The anticipation ramped up and my imagination went into overdrive. All sorts of scenarios were going through my mind. *What if I am rejected? What happens if the recipient has thrown the letter straight into the bin? Is this going to be a complete shock for someone, and how will this person react?* As on many occasions during this search, I felt helpless. I needed to do something to take my mind off things.

CHAPTER EIGHTEEN

Finding Rita

Although it had been a few weeks since I had read Glenda's Inquest Report, it had played on my mind quite a bit. The role played by Rita Fernsby on the day of the overdose puzzled me. How close a relationship did she have with Glenda? Why was she the person to be contacted at that crucial time? She certainly seemed to be aware of the previous attempt at an overdose. Did Glenda confide in her about anything else, such as who the father of the baby was whom she gave up for adoption? If only I could track down Rita Fernsby, I might have a chance of making some sense of all this.

On August Bank Holiday Monday (30 August 2021), I started to search for Rita Fernsby. The first thing to establish was whether she was alive. She was 29 years old when she provided the statement in 1970, and if she was still living, she would be a good age. The first thing I did was to check Facebook. I knew it was an unusual name so wasn't surprised when only two people of that name held profiles. Only one had gone to the trouble of uploading a profile photo. The photo was of an older lady posing next to a statue similar to the Billy Fury statue on Albert Dock, Liverpool. This was a good start as far as I was concerned. The lady I was focusing on had 24 friends listed but didn't appear to have been active on

Facebook since 2017. There were also no clues to indicate it was the Rita I was looking for.

My next move was to dig a little bit deeper into the list of friends. What I soon noticed was that the majority of her friends lived on the west coast of Cumbria or in the vicinity of Littleborough where Glenda lived. This was looking promising. I was pretty sure this was the Rita I was searching for. Then something amazing happened. As I scrolled through her list of her 24 friends again, I recognised the name of one of them. It was a guy called Pyrros, whom I had encountered through my job. In my dealings with him, he was really nice, too. *Oh my goodness, I think I actually know one of Rita Fernsby's Facebook friends! What are the chances of that?* To clarify it was the right Rita Fernsby, I dropped him a quick message: *"Hi Pyrros, I am undertaking some family history research and trying to trace someone called Rita Fernsby. I noticed you have a Facebook friend who goes by that name. The Rita Fernsby I am trying to trace lived near the Rochdale area in 1970. Do you know whether this is the case with your Facebook friend called Rita? Hope it is ok to ask. All the best. Peter."*

The response that came back was as follows: *"Hi Peter, my friend Rita used to live near Rochdale I think, but this was many years ago. She also used to live on the west coast of Cumbria and now she lives abroad. I haven't seen her or spoken to her for a couple of years now. Hope this helps, Pyrros."* Bullseye! I was now pretty confident I had identified the right person. What an amazing stroke of luck to get this confirmed by somebody I knew. It was pretty weird, really. Little did I know it was about to get even weirder!

As Pyrros appeared to have lost contact with Rita, I needed to find somebody within her group of Facebook friends who was still in touch with her and ask whether they would be willing to help me by putting me in touch. I decided the best course of action was to send a generic message to some of her friends asking for help. Interestingly, a couple of them got back to me pretty quickly, informing me that they were still in touch with Rita and that she now lived in Italy. The friend who was the most helpful was called Julie. She acted as an intermediary between me and Rita as messages were exchanged backwards and forwards over the course of that bank holiday afternoon. Initially, Rita was wary of my attempts to get in touch and create a dialogue. Through the intermediary (Julie), she enquired how I knew her, which was the obvious thing to do, as I could have been anybody. My response to Julie was as follows: *"I have been trying to trace my biological family for many years. I have got some information, but not all and I thought Rita may be able to help me. I have only recently come across Rita's name after reading an inquest report linked to a person called Glenda Alice Curruthers. Glenda gave me up for adoption when I was a baby. My understanding was that Glenda and Rita were pretty close, so she might have some information I am not aware of, especially linked to the search for my biological father whom I am yet to trace. If Rita is willing to contact me, it would be really appreciated. Regards, Peter."*

This message seemed to strike a chord, and later on that evening, I received a phone call from a number I didn't recognise. I soon realised the call was coming in from outside the British Isles. I answered it, and on the other end of the line was Rita Fernsby! The conversation was a little bit tense at first. I felt the need to justify who I was and that this wasn't a hoax or a scam. I began by thanking her for agreeing to speak to me and to let her know this was a genuine enquiry. It was difficult to know where to start as there was so much to tell. To try and keep the conversation straightforward, I explained who I was, some brief details about my background, and that I was currently undertaking some research into my biological background. I added that I was hoping she may be able to help me in my search. Fortunately for me, she accepted what I had to say and began to trust me. Soon, we were getting on swimmingly and chatting away as if we had known each other for years. Towards the end of the conversation, she said she was really pleased I had got in touch as she had thought about me on many occasions over the years and prayed things had worked out ok for me. This was heart-warming to hear. I had definitely made the right decision in tracking down Rita Fernsby!

This initial call was followed up by an exchange of family photos via WhatsApp and then a FaceTime call a few days later. This is when I came across a strange coincidence. During the FaceTime call, we chatted about various things, and I happened to ask Rita why she had moved to Italy. Rita explained that her husband had passed away about eight years ago and the house she had previously lived in with her husband was too large once she was on her own. Therefore, she decided to relocate to Italy so she could be near her daughter. The conversation continued as follows. Rita: *"Yes, I moved from a small village on the West Cumbrian coast. I lived there for 24 years. You won't know it; it is called Silecroft. It's not too far from Millom."* Me: *"I know Silecroft alright; it's a village in the district I work in. In fact, the officer I work alongside lives there. She has lived there for 32 years. Here is a photo of her"* (holding up my mobile phone). Rita: *"Yes, I recognise her. That's the lady who lives across from the village shop who has a chess board in her front room on her window ledge."* Me: *"Wow, this is unbelievable. It's an amazing twist of fate. A couple of weeks ago, I came across your name in an inquest report produced in 1970, and you turn out to be a former neighbour of my work colleague who I have spent every day with for the last two years. It's remarkable."*

It was wonderful being able to chat to Rita. This was a connection to Glenda I never thought at all possible. She was interested to hear about the biological search I had been undertaking. She was sad she couldn't assist more. Especially when it came to identifying who my father might be. She hadn't quizzed Glenda at the time as she didn't want to intrude. But listening to my story, she wished she had. Chatting to Rita felt like chatting to another family member, although technically I knew she wasn't. I was really touched when part way through our first FaceTime call, she said: *"I wish I would have kept you myself, but it was difficult as I wasn't family."* This was pretty powerful stuff and I began to sense that this event in 1970 had had an impact on Rita. She had been wondering all these years how things had turned out for me. It was a pleasure to let her know that things were ok. A few days later, she sent me a lovely message via WhatsApp. It was titled: *My Memories of Glenda.* Our conversation had obviously resonated with Rita, and in her own way, she was trying to show me some kindness and provide a little bit more context on Glenda's character, including the challenges she faced. The message read as follows:

Glenda was a beautiful child with very dark hair and brown eyes. She was quiet and shy when we first met. She was going to find life hard because of her disability. She had epilepsy and because of this she needed to be cared for. She was always loved by her cousin Mary, and if she was ill, Mary would take her home from school.

Glenda found life very hard as she grew up, as many employers would sack her when they found out about her illness. This went on for a long time. Also, if she met a boy, again they would all shy away from her. She was beautiful outside and inside and her smile was infectious. It's so sad that the burden of life brought about by her illness robbed her of the happiness she deserved. God bless Glenda.

We agreed to keep in touch, but more importantly, remain friends forever, and we still are.

Chapter Nineteen

Waiting and Hoping

Tracking down Rita Fernsby took my mind off things for a couple of weeks. However, I seemed unable to put the search to the back of my mind knowing that two weeks previously, a letter had arrived on the doormat of somebody who could be my father. Still, there was no response from the team at the research company who were supporting me. As usual, I had to try and stop myself from daydreaming and imagining scenarios of what the recipient of the letter might be going through. As usual, these thoughts were negative rather than positive. Maybe the recipient knew I would try to seek him out one day and dreaded that day coming. It made me angry that I was always being made to wait. Did the recipient not understand that I might have been wondering most of my life who my father was? I was struggling to see this from the recipient's point of view. Who could blame me? I knew the recipient of the letter would be given a month to respond. Another couple of weeks went by and then, on 4 October 2021, I received the following email from the research company. The content of the email wasn't a surprise to me.

Dear Peter,

I am emailing to confirm that no response has yet been received to the initial letter we sent out.

We are therefore sending a follow-up letter. This second letter will be sent via special delivery so we can be confident the correct recipient is receiving our letters.

We allow up to 4 weeks for a reply, but will be in touch once we have any response. If after this period there is no response, and in the assumption the letter is signed for by the correct person, we will send one final letter. This letter is to advise that we will not contact them any further. However, we do stress that we will be forever open to a response should they wish to get in touch.

Over the last few months, especially since the research company had been involved, I had been in good spirits as far as the search was concerned. I was hopeful of an outcome, whatever that might be. I felt that things would turn out ok now the research team were by my side. I didn't feel alone anymore. They were my "knight in shining armour" and we would conquer this together. Receiving this latest email changed things. It reminded me that this search was still far from over. It reminded me that my knight in shining armour was only capable of so much. But most important of all, it reminded me that the recipient of the letter was in control. This reminder affected my mood. My mood deteriorated rapidly. I was snappy with other members of the family. I would take myself off for walks so I could feud on my own. On one occasion, my wife had organised for someone to come to the house to give us some information on having solar panels fitted to the roof. I wasn't in the mood for this and left the house just before the sales representative arrived. I just needed some space to think things through. I was beginning to go backwards again.

Approximately a week before receiving my latest email from the research team, I had received some news which probably contributed to my mood swing. My adopted father had passed away. He had been in a care home for the past five months. The care home was approximately a two-and-a-half-hour drive from where I was living. I was still processing the news of this death in my mind, that someone who had been in my life for 53 years was now no longer here. You get used to having parents in your life, but here I was, both adoptive parents now gone. My adoptive mum died in 2015. The death of my adoptive father was difficult enough to comprehend, but in addition to this, it looked like my potential biological father was deliberately not responding to letters that could help me conclude the ancestral search I had been on for years. Should I begin to finally accept that this was the hand I had been dealt? The next month would be telling.

No news emerged during the month of October. I had spent a chunk of that time away from work that month. This was for a combination of compassionate leave and annual leave. This time away from work gave me more time to think. To ponder my next move. What options did I have available? The obvious ones seemed to be as follows. 1. Continue with the process being used by the research company. Request they send out the third letter and hope the recipient eventually decides to get in touch; 2. Request that they don't send out the third letter; obtain the information established to date and take matters into my own hands by making direct contact with one or both of the brothers identified in the search.

I was a bit deflated to find myself in this situation, to be honest, as it wasn't what I was hoping for. I was obviously hoping that two-way contact would take place with the recipient of the letter, but this hadn't happened. I recalled the conversation I'd had with the representative from the research company a few months earlier, who explained that their company had a 94% success rate in helping

On holiday in Scotland. Not sure what to make of this sailing malarkey.

people trace family and relatives. I was now questioning what this actually meant. Did it mean that 94% of people were successfully linked together? If so, it was looking pretty slim at this stage that I would be one of those successes. I should have known this might be the case. Nothing had been straightforward or easy with this search.

Following a rather tense conversation with a member of staff from the research company in mid-November, I agreed to a third and final letter being sent out. I was informed that the team who were supporting me had reviewed my case at one of their recent meetings and that the final letter template being sent was to be slightly amended to provide clarity to the recipient as to why they were receiving the letter. It was hoped this would trigger a response. On this occasion, we agreed that the recipient would be given a maximum of two weeks to respond. Again, I asked myself why the first two letters had been ignored and whether this final letter would make any difference. I wasn't that hopeful. All I could do was wait.

I was used to that, though; it was something I was accustomed to. It was going to be a long two weeks.

My prediction for the next two weeks wasn't wrong. It was dragging. Each day seemed to last longer than the previous one. I constantly checked my phone for missed calls and emails, just in case the research company had tried to contact me. Alas, there was nothing doing. I'd not felt this kind of frustration since I was a child. I recalled the countdowns to my birthday and Christmas, and when time seemed to stand still. I guess I was "wishing my life away", which was probably not the right thing to do for the simple reason that none of us can guarantee that tomorrow will come.

On Tuesday, 7 December 2021, the research company sent across an email explaining they were sorry, but they had not received a response to the third and final letter they had sent out. As a result, Gordon Ings was going to share my family tree with me and produce a report on the work that he had completed. It was confirmed I would have this by the end of that week. The disappointment and hurt linked to the previous letters being ignored soon dissipated. A touch of excitement was now in the air but mingled with apprehension. In a couple of days, I was about to receive a report containing the names of two individuals, one of whom was my biological father. I was creeping ever closer to the truth. I was also about to lose my comfort blanket and would be once again on my own!

CHAPTER TWENTY

Biological Family Revealed

Thursday, 9 December 2021 was a momentous day. My DNA Investigation Report arrived by email. It was sent across by Gordon Ings. Initially, I felt sick when I saw the email, but my curiosity soon displaced any queasiness. This was the moment I had been looking forward to since commissioning the research team to act on my behalf and undertake the search. Cautiously I opened the email, then clicked on the attachment titled Search Report. I skimmed it as I was keen to reach the page where it stated who my potential biological father was. On reaching page 5, it confirmed I was biologically linked to a family called Fairclough. More specifically, I was likely to be the son of a **HAROLD FAIRCLOUGH** or a **THOMAS FAIRCLOUGH**, with the report strongly indicating that **THOMAS FAIRCLOUGH was my biological father**! I stared at the screen. I was dancing for joy inside, but I didn't let it show. This information was backed up with scientific evidence, and nobody could take that away from me or question it. I couldn't stop reading the detail and read it over and over again. I was on cloud nine as I knew this was the furthest point I had reached in the search to date. I also felt a sense of relief. The tension floated away like a black cloud on a windy day. Hopefully, it was only a matter of time now before I concluded the search. It should be plain sailing from here, I thought.

Gordon Ings had kept his word and the report he sent contained the investigation he had undertaken step by step. It also included diagrams of the paternal family tree to help me visualise the linkages from generation to generation.

In summary, the report read as follows:

Objective:

To identify your biological father and any living relative through DNA.

You were born Colin Curruthers in 1968 in Littleborough, Rochdale, Greater Manchester.

Your mother was Glenda Alice Curruthers.

You were adopted and therefore had no information about your biological father.

Search details:

Your DNA results provided a number of matches who we believed to be paternal. The closest matches are detailed below:

Jennifer Myers 1.53% (114cM) of shared DNA – 23&me database

Lorna Clapham 1.29% of shared DNA – 23&me database

At this level of centimorgans (cMs) we believed the most likely relationship between yourself, Jennifer & Lorna would be a second cousin once removed. Which means they would be second cousins to your father.

Research into Jennifer Myers' family tree:

As Jennifer was based in Ontario, Canada, we were looking at some connection within her ancestry which tied back to the UK. We were able to establish that her paternal grandmother was Eliza Buckle (1888-1968) born in Whitworth, Rossendale, Lancashire.

Research into Lorna Clapham's family tree:

Lorna was based in Alabama, USA, so again we were looking for some family connection back to the UK.

We were able to establish that Lorna's maternal grandmother was Fanny Buckle (1902-1997) born in Rochdale, Greater Manchester.

Further investigation found that Fanny & Eliza Buckle were sisters with their parents being Richard Buckle (1836-1911) & Elizabeth Constantine (1863-1932). We were now confident that we had found the common ancestors and that your father would most likely be the grandson of one of Fanny & Eliza's siblings. The majority of the Buckle family appeared to have moved to either Canada or Alabama; there was only one branch that remained in the UK.

At this point we also received new DNA matches on your Ancestry account who we believed were paternal. Gary Fairclough was the closest match by far who shares 12% and 803cM of DNA with yourself. At this level of centimorgans the most likely relationship between you and Gary would be first cousins. Which meant one of his uncles has to be your father.

Research into Gary Fairclough's family tree:

We then built out Gary's family tree. We were able to establish that his great-grandmother was Emma Buckle (1883-1935), who was the sister of Eliza and Fanny Buckle. This gave us even more confidence that your father was part of the Buckle family. Gary's family tree clarified that he has two uncles, Harold Fairclough (b. 1931) and Thomas Fairclough (b. 1942).

We were confident that Thomas Fairclough is your biological father as he is a similar age to your mother and also has never married. We were able to locate a current address for Thomas. This concluded the investigation.

Over the next 24 hours, I started to think more about the family to which the DNA Investigation Search Report indicated I was biologically linked. Nobody with the surname Fairclough had cropped up in this search before. Naturally, I started to imagine what they were like; I couldn't help it. I was also aware that I needed a strategy to get closer to the family and establish the truth about who my biological father was. The DNA Investigation Search Report, along with the family tree uploaded onto my Ancestry DNA account, showed that Thomas Fairclough had three siblings named Harold, Eric and Josephine. As far as I could tell, they were all still living, apart from Eric, who died in 2010. The family tree also confirmed that there was a generation of siblings below them, with Harold and Eric both having children. Thomas Fairclough wasn't identified as having any children, though. I decided that my greatest chance of success was to try to make contact with a member, or members, of the family from this generation to see whether anybody knew anything about my situation. With no blueprint to follow, it was the only idea I could come up with. I felt excited, though.

CHAPTER TWENTY ONE

The Truth, Finally...

To try and make contact with family members of either Harold or Eric, my chosen strategy was to revert to the Facebook groups I had used earlier in the year. Although he couldn't provide exact addresses, Gordon Ings had confirmed that Harold Fairclough and Thomas Fairclough still lived in the North West of England. It therefore made sense that some members of the Fairclough family might still have connections to the area in which they grew up and had joined Facebook groups to keep in touch. The preferred Facebook group I re-joined was Littleborough People – Past & Present. Within 24 hours, I had been accepted back onto the group. I knew I had to be vague with my post as this was a sensitive subject I was dealing with. The last thing I needed was to get people's backs up or distress anyone.

My post read as follows: *"I am researching my family tree and members of this group have been very helpful and supportive in the past. I am now researching a different branch of the family and am interested to know more about the Fairclough family who are thought to originate from the Littleborough or Rochdale area. Family members I am aware of are Josephine Fairclough (born 1930), Harold Fairclough (born 1931), Eric Fairclough (born 1932) and Thomas Fairclough (born 1942).*

I would be grateful if anyone with connections to the family would get in touch as you may be able to help me."

Within a few hours, I had a response to the Facebook post. I was contacted by one of Eric Fairclough's daughters. We exchanged a couple of messages and agreed to speak on the telephone as I thought it would be much quicker to explain my reason for getting in touch. I knew it wouldn't be an easy conversation, and I couldn't foresee how it would go. Initially, I explained who I was and that my enquiry was genuine. I went on to explain I had been searching for my biological father for many years and more recently my search had led me to the Fairclough family. More specifically, using my DNA, it had been confirmed that I am genetically linked to either Harold Fairclough or Thomas Fairclough. Her response to this wasn't that positive initially. As the eldest daughter of Eric, she explained she was generally abreast of family affairs but knew nothing about what I was referring to. She went on to say that although her immediate family were close, she didn't keep in touch with members of the wider family such as Harold's siblings (her cousins). She was also unwilling to give any details of individuals in the wider family who might be able to help me. During the conversation, I was also told to be grateful for the family I had and was asked whether it was worth digging up the past. This conversation with Eric's daughter lasted about 30 minutes and I made little progress. She did, however, after some gentle persuasion, agree to speak to another member of the Fairclough family who she thought might be able to assist. This was someone whom she had seen recently at a family funeral and was in touch with. She said she couldn't guarantee this person would assist me, but I thanked her for her time, nonetheless.

As soon as the phone call was over, I reflected on how it had gone. Poorly, was the best way to describe it. I naively thought that she would have been a little more sympathetic and welcoming. She was certainly more defensive than I anticipated and demonstrated a sense of protectiveness towards her immediate and wider family. I suppose I shouldn't blame her. Here she was, chatting to a complete stranger who claimed he was, in effect, her cousin.

I realised I had, perhaps, underestimated the challenge I was facing. Although I had picked up the baton from the research company, and I was in the last leg of the search, I still had further work to do. Somehow, I needed to broker a relationship with a member of the Fairclough family who was willing to play a mediator role and speak to Harold or Thomas on my behalf. Following the phone call, I now realised that my chances of success would be higher if I could connect with one of Harold's siblings, rather than those of Eric. This was my best option as my understanding was that Thomas didn't have any children, or so I thought.

For the next 24 hours after this latest phone call, I felt really low and frustrated. I had not experienced feeling like this for many months, certainly not while the research company had been involved, anyway. I was angry that I had lowered my guard and had adopted the mindset that this stage of the search would be plain sailing. How stupid had I been? I should have known better. I didn't see any positives, following the telephone call, just the negatives. I was wondering what to do next when I noticed there was another response to my Facebook post. The message was brief but read: *"I might be able to assist you"* and was sent by someone called Carol Fairclough. I did a quick scan of the family tree but couldn't see anyone of that name. It didn't matter; here was somebody else willing to talk to me.

Once again, I knew it would be easier to speak directly with the person, so I asked whether it would be ok to call her. Her returning messages were not quick, so it wasn't until the next evening that I was able to make the call. As before, I explained who I was and that my enquiry was genuine. I went on to explain I had been searching for my biological father for many years and more recently my search had led me to the Fairclough family. She explained that she was one of Harold Fairclough's children.

It soon became evident during our conversation that she was aware of my backstory, and I realised that my search was being discussed behind the scenes amongst the wider family. She was very defensive of her father, Harold, and clarified that he was not involved in this situation. She mentioned she had spoken to him earlier that day and that he was aware of an incident involving his brother Thomas Fairclough, many years ago. Her father explained that Thomas, who was married at the time (even though I had been advised in the information that he was unmarried) and whose wife was pregnant and expecting their third child, had an affair, and the young lady in question fell pregnant. Therefore, he was in a situation where two women he was linked to were pregnant at the same time. I sat and listened intently, taking in every word she said. My mind was racing, though. I thought, *no wonder Thomas wasn't named on my adoption records.* This would have been a massive cover-up job and nobody would have wanted to carry the can for it. There would have been too much at stake in terms of his marriage to announce he had been in another relationship. If this version of events was true, and it seemed to make sense the more I thought about it, surely the person that Thomas had an affair with was Glenda. It had to be, hadn't it? Therefore, after all these years of searching, I had finally got my man. **Thomas Fairclough was my biological father.** Hats off to Gordon Ings; he was bang on with his research and prediction.

I thanked Carol for her help and stressed how important the information was to me. What would be really useful and would save me time in the long run was if she could provide me with the name of the town Thomas Fairclough lived in. I knew that it was unlikely she would provide his address, so pushed for the name of the town without trying to sound desperate. She was reluctant to provide this but hinted he was closer to where I lived than I thought. My mind went into overdrive, and I asked whether he lived in Cumbria. If this was the case, it would be really spooky. Again, she clammed up. Eventually, after I'd made the request several times, she said she would consult with her sister and then get back to me. Although I didn't manage to get the information, I realised I had to keep on good terms with her, so I accepted this option as an alternative.

When the call ended, I sat there in silence and absorbed what I had just heard. For a moment, I tried to put myself in Glenda's shoes and tried to understand the predicament she found herself in. It must have been an extremely emotional time and would have certainly been a taboo subject. Carrying the child of a married man, and more alarmingly, a married man whose wife was also pregnant! Who could she discuss it with? She would have needed a network of support around her, but I bet that wasn't the case. She would have been in turmoil with nowhere to turn. Suddenly, these thoughts were interrupted by a call on my mobile phone. Surprisingly, it was Carol Fairclough again. *"I've had a word with my sister; Thomas Fairclough lives in Lancaster,"* she said. I once again thanked her for her help and told her how much this meant to me. So, in the space of 45 minutes, with the help of Carol Fairclough, I had almost certainly identified my biological father and discovered the town he lived in. I was thrilled with the progress made, especially after the lows I had experienced 48 hours earlier. The pendulum was now unquestionably swinging in my favour.

CHAPTER TWENTY TWO

Reaching Out to My Father

Based on the two conversations I'd had with members of the Fairclough family, it was clear that Thomas was detached from his siblings and they rarely communicated with him, let alone met him face to face. Some of them hadn't seen him for years, and he hadn't recently turned up to the funeral of his sister-in-law (Harold's wife). Therefore, unless other members of the family came forward, I was now on my own. The hope of having an intermediary in place was fading fast.

I thought about what to do next. My options were limited. I decided that I would write him a letter and ask him to make contact with me. If that didn't work, and it might not, based on recent experiences, I would cold call at his property. I know this was a risky strategy that I had carried out before, but as Del Boy Trotter of *Only Fools and Horses* used to say: "He who dares, wins." If the second option was to happen, and he didn't want to know or shut the door in my face or something, I would have to accept this and reluctantly bring the search to an end. This was the plan I had mentally committed to.

To move the plan forward, I had to establish Thomas's address as I would need this for the letter. I would also need the address if the letter option didn't work and I ended up cold calling. A work colleague of mine had mentioned 192.com to me a few days previously. Although I was hesitant to part with any more money on this search, I reluctantly paid £20.00 and opened an account with 192.com for a limited period, and with limited searches. I was praying that the information established so far, that is, his name, town of residence and year of birth, would be enough to identify his address. My initial search on 192.com drew a blank and stated "No search results". How could that be? Surely there must be a mistake. I was told he lived in Lancaster. The second time I input the data, I decided to type in Preston as place of residence instead of Lancaster. Bingo: this time, two search results were revealed. There appeared to be two people called Thomas Fairclough living just on the outskirts of Lancaster. I was 99 per cent sure it was one of these, but I still needed to clarify which one it was. I recalled what Carol Fairclough had told me during a previous conversation, that Thomas had a partner. Looking at the addresses in front of me again, it was possible to see who else resided at each address. It confirmed that only one of the addresses had more than one person living in it. The occupiers were a Thomas Fairclough and a Bridget Whittaker. They had both lived at this address for a number of years. This had to be it. This was where I was going to send the letter.

A few months earlier, I was asked by staff at the research company to draft a personal statement in readiness for their letters being responded to. I had done this soon after they had requested it and they had approved the content. I therefore decided to use this template for the letter I was now ready to draft. On Tuesday, 21 December 2021, I posted my letter to Thomas Fairclough and then waited. It contained the following information:

Dear Thomas

My name is Peter Jackson, born 13th May 1968 to Glenda Alice Curruthers, who previously lived at 196 Mayo Lane, Littleborough. I was adopted in 1968 when I was approximately six months old. I know I was given up for adoption under difficult circumstances, but I am unaware of how much knowledge you have of this.

Recently, I have been supported by an organisation who have assisted me as I attempt to trace my birth parents. Sadly, Glenda is no longer living as she passed away in 1970. Using DNA evidence and family tree analysis, it has been confirmed that I am first generation biologically linked to the Fairclough family, and more specifically, as a son of either you or your brother Harold (born 1931). After speaking to members of the Fairclough family, I understand this is likely to be you. I understand you were involved in an extramarital relationship in 1967 and the lady in question fell pregnant. Therefore, it is extremely likely you are my biological father. If you weren't aware, I understand that this may come as a shock and may take some getting used to.

I am now 53. I am married with two daughters aged 19 and 12, and we live in Keswick, Cumbria. My eldest daughter has just completed her first year at university. I work in local government and my wife is a nurse. I have enclosed a photo of me for your interest.

I hope to understand my family history further and therefore I am keen to meet you. I recognise this is a sensitive subject and I do not intend to upset you or change your life in any way. I also do not want to intrude or interfere in your life. I would be happy just to meet you briefly, as this would allow me to have closure after such a long time wondering about my heritage.

Please could you contact me on the contact details listed below so we can arrange to meet up? I would be grateful if you could contact me over the next week.

Kind regards
Peter

CHAPTER TWENTY THREE

A Christmas Miracle

For whatever reason, Thomas hadn't responded to three letters sent by the research company. Therefore, my letter was sent in hope, rather than in anticipation. The week the letter was posted coincided with a couple of long-awaited hospital appointments. Also, my daughter and her partner were coming to visit us for a couple of days. This distracted me somewhat and took my focus away from any impending phone calls. I had resigned myself to the thought that nothing was going to happen this side of Christmas. Then suddenly, something remarkable happened. On the evening of Christmas Eve, my mobile phone rang. It was a Lancaster dialling code. Bloody hell! This must be Thomas Fairclough! I stared at the phone in amazement. I was taken by surprise, and I didn't pick it up. I'd been searching all this time and here was my chance to talk to him and I didn't take it. This was presuming it was who I thought it was on the other end of the line. I wanted to be prepared for this conversation and I wasn't. The phone rang out and a voicemail had been left. I quickly called 121, and sure enough, it was in relation to Thomas Fairclough, only it wasn't him. It was a woman ringing on his behalf. I assumed this was his partner. She explained that Thomas had received a letter and that he would like to speak to me, and could I ring back when I was free. The message was concise and calm.

I explained to my wife what had happened. She insisted I ring back straight away. I had other ideas as I needed to mentally prepare myself for returning the call. I gave myself half an hour then rang back. I could feel my heart pumping faster and I paced across the room. I planned in my mind what to say and what not to say. This was my chance, and I didn't want to balls it up. The lady who had left the message answered. Her telephone voice was very clear, and she was very polite. I explained who I was and thanked her for calling me. The lady asked if I wanted to speak to Thomas. I said that I did and she passed the phone across to him. *Here goes*, I thought. *You are about to achieve what you have been longing to do for many, many years: to actually speak to your biological father.* A summary of the conversation is as follows:

"Hello Thomas, Thanks for calling me; I'm really grateful. I sent you a letter earlier this week. I hope it explains the reasons for wanting to get in touch. I've been searching for you for quite a long time. You are a pretty difficult guy to track down. Anyway, I've found you now." [Me]

"Yes Peter, I have received your letter. I didn't realise you had been looking for me. I'm really sorry to hear about your biological mother. I didn't realise." (He was referring to her death in 1970.) [Thomas]

"As I mentioned in the letter, Thomas, this has been such a long search for me, and I would really like to have some closure. I'd like to come and see you, if that is ok with you? Maybe a chat over a cup of coffee. I want to make it clear that I don't want to upset you in any way or intrude into your life. This isn't my intention. It's just so I can get a better understanding of what went on all those years ago." [Me]

"Yes, that's fine." [Thomas]

"When would be a good time to come and see you? Between Christmas and New Year or would you rather wait until after New Year?" [Me]

"I'd prefer to wait until the New Year, if that's ok, as I have some hospital appointments arranged for that week." [Thomas]

"Ok, I'll ring you after New Year and we can arrange a date and time. I would just like to thank you again for making contact with me. For me, this is the best Christmas present I have ever had. Hope you have a lovely Christmas." [Peter]

As the call ended, I had to pinch myself. Had this actually happened? Had I just spoken to my biological father for the first time? Also, why was the conversation so amicable? I was used to rejection. I was used to barriers and obstacles being put in my way. He didn't question anything in the letter or deny he was my father! He seemed to accept it all. No wonder I had to pinch myself as I wasn't used to this reaction. He didn't even mind when I asked to meet up with him. It was like taking candy from a baby. Maybe the "adoption gods" thought I had been tormented enough on this journey and wanted to give me an easy ride as I entered the final furlong. Well, I was all for an easy ride; besides, I didn't think I had the stomach for any more challenges. That evening, I relaxed with a couple of beers and let what had happened sink in. It was a Christmas Eve I was never, ever going to forget. I was beginning to understand what closure felt like. Closure felt great.

The feel-good factor remained with me across Christmas and New Year. Sometimes I had to tell myself that the conversation had taken place on Christmas Eve and that it wasn't a dream I had experienced. Although I was on a high, I couldn't escape those moments of doubt, the fear that he might ring up and do a U-turn about me visiting him. Thankfully, that conversation never took place, and in a second phone call just after New Year, we agreed on the date and time for a face-to-face visit, which was to be Sunday, 9 January, at 1.00 pm.

During the week leading up to the visit, I tried really hard to distract myself. Even though I had returned to work after Christmas, it wasn't easy remaining focused. I wasn't surprised about this. At the end of the day, I was about to meet someone and hopefully find out information that had eluded me for a significant chunk of my life. This was massive for me. I was well aware that the conversation we were due to have in a few days' time might not be pleasant for either of us, though. He might find it difficult, embarrassing, and be full of remorse or regrets. I couldn't predict how he was going to react. I also needed to take on board that he might not remember things either. After all, from the brief conversation we had on Christmas Eve, it sounded as if he had only met her twice. Also, their acquaintance took place over half a century ago.

The closer I got to the day of the meeting, the more questions I had in my mind. I wondered how to pitch the meeting. Should it be formal or more relaxed? If I only got one bite of the cherry at this, then I needed to obtain as much information from this one meeting as I could. If he wanted to stay in touch, how would I feel about that? I also considered whether I should take photos along with me, not only of Glenda but also of my family. Should I ask for photos of him, particularly when he was younger? What would they think of me? And what questions would they ask me? What would Glenda have made of all this? Would she have been pleased I was meeting Thomas? Would she be proud of me and the fact that I never gave up on this relentless search? I was going into the unknown and would just have to wait and see how the meeting went.

CHAPTER TWENTY FOUR

The Greatest Day

Sunday, 9 December 2022 arrived, and I was up early. I normally go metal detecting on Sunday mornings, but not today. I decided to go out for an early morning walk so I could think in more detail about the day ahead. It was dark when I set off. During the walk, I cast my mind back to just before Christmas last year when, on the same footpath, the long, tormenting search got the better of me and I broke down and burst into tears. This morning's walk was exactly the opposite. I was striding along, very assured, and rid of all that apprehension and frustration that had been a burden on me for so long. I had noticed that since receiving the phone call from Thomas Fairclough on Christmas Eve, my head felt far different than it had in a very long time. The fuzziness, the headaches and the inability to think straight had faded, leaving me with a fresh, unclogged head and a positive mindset. I didn't realise how terrible I had been feeling and what a struggle each day had been until this change had taken place. I had to admit this new feeling inside my head was great. Towards the end of the walk, the radio station I was plugged into played Greatest Day by Take That. I smiled as I listened to the lyrics: *"today, this could be, the greatest day of our lives"* sung by Gary Barlow and co. They could be right.

The plan was to drive to Lancaster for 1.00 pm but drop off my wife and younger daughter at my elder daughter's place as she was at university not too far from where Thomas lived, and they had planned a shopping trip. I would go off to my meeting with Thomas and then pick them up on the way home. Although I was apprehensive, I was conscious that I had had a dress rehearsal for this about 12 months earlier when I went to meet Derek Forsyth in a supermarket car park on the outskirts of Rochdale. I managed to get through that unscathed, so surely this would be a breeze. The only difference between this meeting and the last meeting was that this time, there was no need to pack a DNA test kit in the boot of my car as I knew exactly who I was going to meet. My biological father!

According to my wife, I was very quiet during the journey to Lancaster. I wasn't surprised as I felt nauseous and was playing out in my mind how the meeting would pan out later that day. The property I was looking for was in a residential park just off the A6. The area was modern, with homeowners having access to leisure facilities, shopping, golf, fishing, birdwatching and beautiful fell, river and canal walks. I turned into the park and soon found the property. It was eleven minutes past one, so I was slightly later than planned. A lady with white hair waved at me through the window of the property and signalled me to come in. I parked my car just behind theirs on the short narrow drive. Unsurprisingly, I was nervous, but at the same time, I didn't feel under any pressure as it wasn't me who was under the microscope. I was here to find answers. I was also still buzzing for actually having made it to this point on the journey. It was a minor miracle, really, and I was secretly proud of myself.

On entering the property, I soon realised how small it was inside. I made my own way through to the main living area, rather than being greeted at the door and escorted. I thought this was a bit strange, but I just went with it. My heart was pounding as I opened the door to what was a really small living room. This is it, I thought to myself. Thomas was sat at the opposite end of the room, but the room was that small, he was only a few yards away. As I moved towards the two-seater settee to sit down, Thomas reached out to shake hands. I noticed he avoided eye contact, but I was ok about that. This was a positive start as far as I was concerned. The lady with the white hair introduced herself as Bridget. She asked whether I would like a drink and a piece of cake as she had been baking earlier that morning. Whether she had been baking on my account I did not know. She scurried off to the kitchen and was soon back with a cup of coffee and a piece of fruit cake.

Once we were all settled, I thanked them for meeting me and explained that all I hoped to get out of the meeting was to establish the facts of what had happened back in 1967/8 as this would help me bring closure to the search I had been on. I explained that I had been searching for information on my biological lineage for some time and that for the last few months I had been supported by a research company linked to the television programme Long Lost Family. Providing my DNA, combined with their expertise in genealogy, had led me to the Fairclough family, and either Thomas or Harold was more than likely my biological father. I asked whether Thomas had received any letters from the research company. Bridget explained that Thomas didn't read any mail that came through the post to him and that she had to deal with all his correspondence. She recalled reading one letter from the research company but said she didn't understand it, so she passed it across to her daughter to have a look at, who then forgot all about it. I tried not to get annoyed by this admission, as I had experienced quite an anxious few weeks waiting for someone to respond to these letters. I didn't realise they had been simply disregarded. They did, however, explain that the personal letter I sent out just before Christmas was very clear and to the point.

I went on to explain that I didn't want to dig up the past and cause any upset for anyone. I wasn't there to interfere or to bulldoze into their lives, either. To their credit, they both were unfazed and seemed happy to chat about it. I remember thinking, *this is going well*.

To start the ball rolling, I got out some photos I had brought along with me. These were photos of me at different stages of my life and photos of my wife and children. I wanted to try and put them at ease and show them that I was just a general guy who was getting on with life the best he could, and that I was doing ok. The photos triggered some questions about my life, which kept the conversation going and which I was happy to answer.

Whilst Thomas was scanning the photos, I looked at him in a bit more detail. He was sat in his armchair but was resting his legs on a buffet. I sensed that he spent a lot of time in that chair, and based on his physique, my assumption was that he didn't take much physical exercise, either. This became apparent later on that afternoon when he outlined the numerous health conditions he had suffered from over the years. He was wearing tracksuit bottoms and a grey sweatshirt sporting an England football badge, which seemed to have seen better days. Thinking back, he was exactly the opposite of Derek Forsyth, whom I had met 12 months previously, who appeared to be taking care of himself and had pride in his appearance. I asked if they wanted to keep the photos and they seemed keen.

Before the meeting, I couldn't be sure whether this was going to be a one-off meeting with Thomas or whether further visits were to take place. With that in mind, I had come prepared and had written a list of questions beforehand to which I was keen to get answers. Before diving into the questions, I thought I had better check with Bridget how she felt about this, as the questions were likely to be linked to Thomas's past and probably to a time before he knew her. She explained she was fine about it. For the next few minutes, the conversation was as follows:

"How did you meet Glenda? Was it socially or through work?" [Me]

"I only met Glenda once, and that was at a dance hall. I think she had just returned from a camping holiday, possibly in Wales. We hit it off that night and one thing led to another, as they say. Other than that night, I only came across her on one more occasion. It was about six months later. She came into a pub I was in. I could see she was pregnant, and when we were chatting about it, she said, 'Don't worry, Thomas, the baby isn't yours." [Thomas]

"Ok, so you only met her once. I didn't realise that." [Me] (I was thinking, wow, that was quick. They didn't mess about there, did they?)

"Were you in a relationship with somebody else on the night you met Glenda at the dance hall? Other family members I have spoken to suggest you were married at the time." [Me]

"I can't remember. I think I may have been going through a divorce at the time. Looking back, I got married far too young." [Thomas]

"Do you have any other children apart from me? Are any of them aware that I exist?" [Me]

"Yes, I have three children. Two girls and a boy. The boy died, though. They are not aware you exist." [Thomas]

"What are your daughters called?" [Me]

"They are called Judith and Lesley. Thomas hasn't been in contact with his children for quite a long time now. [Bridget answered on Thomas's behalf.]

"Do you mind if I ask how your son died?" [Me]

We are not sure. We think he may have been struggling for some time. He would have been about 50 years old." [Thomas]

"How old was Glenda when she died?" [Bridget]

"She was only 26." [Me]

"That's really young. Was she ill or something?" [Thomas]

"No, I'm afraid she took her own life. She was struggling to cope with her epilepsy and giving me up and everything. She tried to end her life soon after I was born, but she survived. The second time, she did the job properly. [Me] (Part of me was wanting to get a subtle message across, that due to these moments of lust, there had been a negative knock-on effect and this had impacted various people.)

At this point in the conversation, I realised that the missing pieces of the jigsaw were now in place. I wasn't entirely sure how accurate the information was, but I accepted it. I didn't want to upset the ambience by probing further or nit-picking at what had been said. I was conscious that some of the questions I had on my sheet I didn't need to ask now as they were irrelevant. These were questions such as: How long were you in a relationship with Glenda? What did you do when you found out she was pregnant? Can you tell me whether you were told about the pregnancy? If so, who told you? What kind of support did you give her (if any)? Did she ask for support from you? Did you have any feelings for her? Can you tell me how you felt about her? Did you see me when I was born? Derek Forsyth and George Robson were named in my adoption file. Did you know them or have knowledge of these men? Did you know that they were named? Why did that happen? Why weren't you named? Have you ever wondered about me over the years or thought about trying to search me out? What happened to your first wife? What was she called?

We chatted about other things over the course of the afternoon. Thomas told me that he'd suffered from lots of health issues over the last few years. He'd had a nervous breakdown in the mid-eighties which resulted in his not wanting to leave the house for a number of months. He explained he was a trained painter and decorator and was self-employed. One day, he fell off a ladder and seriously injured his leg. He said he suffered from arthritis quite badly. It started in the leg he had damaged when he came off the ladder and now affected the whole of his upper body too. He mentioned that his dad had died of bowel cancer, but I didn't ask when that was. He was also a smoker, but he didn't have a cigarette whilst I was there. This was all interesting stuff to listen to, especially as I had started with arthritis in my left knee a few years ago, which had worsened. It begged the question of whether any of these conditions were hereditary and whether I or my children could potentially suffer from them too.

Bridget, on the other hand, was fit as a fiddle. She was in good shape for an 88-year-old and explained she could still walk 10 miles a day. A few years ago, at the grand old age of 82, she trekked 500 miles with her granddaughter across Spain, in just under a month. I could see she was immensely proud of her achievement.

They asked me about my adoption and whether I had had a good adoption. I didn't want to go into detail about this, so I opted for the safe response and explained that my adoption had been ok, thanks. Interestingly, Bridget's stance on this was that adopted people generally end up having happy lives. It wasn't the time to get into a debate about this, and I was non-committal, although I did think to myself, *how wrong you are on that score, as many of us are damaged goods.*

We may have talked about more general stuff too, but emotions were running high, and thinking back, it is a bit of a blur. I think I recall them saying that they weren't interested in technology. Also, that they used to holiday abroad quite a lot. I couldn't believe how fast the time went by. I looked at my watch and realised I had been there for nearly two hours. I didn't want to outstay my welcome and began to leave. This triggered a question from Bridget: "Do you want to see us again?" I knew, just from the brief time I had spent with Thomas, that there hadn't been a "connection". Also, based on what I had seen, and what he had told me, he didn't seem the type you could build a rapport with. After all, he seemed to have disconnected from the three children he had from his first marriage, although I don't fully understand the circumstances behind this. As far as I was concerned, I had achieved my objective by tracing my biological father and filled in the gaps in my knowledge. My desire had not been to build a relationship with my biological father as part of this quest. With all this running through my mind, and not wanting to appear rude, I confirmed with them that they had my contact details and that I was happy to keep in touch with them. I wasn't going to commit to anything else at this stage. Thomas responded by saying, "Yes, next time you are out this way, call in." I wasn't exactly sure what to make of this comment.

It was Bridget who showed me out. Just as I left, she handed me a homemade jar of Damson jam. She also gave me a carrier bag and said, "These are the photos and the diary I kept from my trek across Spain. I don't normally lend them to people, but I trust you. I do want them back, though." Maybe this was her way of enticing me back, I don't know.

As I slowly drove away, Thomas was still sat in his chair but waved at me through the window. I left the residential park and joined the A6 as I headed back to my wife and daughters. My emotions were all over the place. I was amazed that I had completed my mission. The adrenalin was now fading fast, and I was mentally drained. Still, my mind wandered. Maybe it was due to being exhausted, but part of me was consumed by sadness. I had been on this relentless journey alone, as my biological mother had not been around to help provide the answers to my questions as only she could. Although the question of paternity had been the main focus of this search, understanding her rationale for giving me up would also have been comforting. Giving up your baby must be one of the hardest things a woman can do. Yet for reasons known only to her, this decision was made, leaving me to rely on what was coldly stated in the files sourced from the Social Services office. This information could never relay the emotion of that time.

Writing about this search has certainly been a cathartic experience. I sincerely hope it will give others a glimmer of hope, if nothing else, on their personal quests. On reflection, it has been a remarkable journey to have been on, in terms of its uniqueness. I've certainly left no stone unturned to reveal the truth. I also doubt that another human being will tread this same unconventional path. Neither will they experience the poignancy of the wreath in the hallway on the anniversary of their mother's death. I wonder if Glenda would have been proud of me for completing this mammoth search to finally uncover the truth. I do hope so.

Printed in Great Britain
by Amazon